# Hands-On Python Mastery

Step by Step Tutorial

**G. Prabu Kanna**
*Senior Assistant Professor,*
*School of Computing Science Engineering*
*and Artificial Intelligence (SCAI),*
*VIT Bhopal University,*
*Sehore, Madhya Pradesh, India.*

**S. Devaraju**
*Senior Assistant Professor,*
*School of Computing Science Engineering*
*and Artificial Intelligence (SCAI),*
*VIT Bhopal University,*
*Sehore, Madhya Pradesh, India.*

**Sathish Kumar L**
*Senior Assistant Professor,*
*School of Computing Science and Engineering (SCOPE),*
*VIT Bhopal University,*
*Sehore, Madhya Pradesh, India*

# EDITORS PROFILE

 **_Dr. Prabu Kanna G_** _is an Senior Assistant Professor Grade - II in the school of Computing Science and Engineering, VIT Bhopal University, Madhya Pradesh. He has received his Ph.D in 2019 and has done his Master degree in Information Technology in 2011 from Kalasalingam Academy of Research and Education. He has served different academic and administrative roles in various institutions since 2011. Dr. Prabu Kanna G has several publications, in peer reviewed International and National journals with high impact factor. He has contributed a number of Conferences, Workshops and Faculty Development Program. His area of research includes Cloud Computing, Big Data, Artificial Intelligence, and Machine Learning._

 **_Dr. S. Devaraju_** _is an Senior Assistant Professor in the School of Computing Science and Engineering (SCSE) at VIT Bhopal University. He received his Doctorate from Anna University, an M.Phil in Computer Science from Periyar University and an MCA in Computer Applications from Periyar University. He has an academic experience of 19 years and 2 years of Industry at various levels. He has 20 publications in peer reviewed International/National journals and has 20 publications in various International/National Conferences. Dr. Devaraju has organized/Attended a number of Conferences, Workshops and FDP. Dr.Devaraju has published 2 patents, 5 Book Chapters and Reviewer for various reputed Journals and Conferences. He is a lifetime member of IACSITand ISTE, India. His area of research includes Network Security, Intrusion Detection, Soft Computing, and Wireless Communication._

**_Dr. Sathish Kumar L._** _is working as a Senior Assistant Professor in the Gaming Division, School of Computing Science and Engineering, VIT Bhopal University. Dr. Sathish completed his Ph.D., in Computer Science and Engineering at Alagappa University, Karaikudi. He has 12 years of academic experience and more than 35 research publications in refereed international and national journals and conferences. Dr. Sathish has two international patents and one design patent to his credit and has received two awards for his research and academic contributions. He has published six textbooks entitled Desktop Publishing, Desktop Publishing Second Edition, Artificial Intelligence, Data Communication and Networking, Java Programming, and Think by Python. He has completed consulting project work in "Text Archaeology with Tagged Indian Languages" with Asia University, Taiwan. He is taking E-Learning courses that are Mobile Game Development Basics, Intermediate, and Advanced. He is a reviewer for leading SCI and Scopus-indexed journals like Wireless Networks Journal, Springer, Alexandria Engineering Journal, Elsevier, IET Electronics Letters, and Ad-hoc Sensor Wireless Networks Journal, Old City Publishing, etc. He has been a resource person/session chair for a number of international conferences. He is a lifetime member of IEEE and a life member of IAENG. He is an active researcher in the fields of medical image processing, deep learning, machine learning, and data science._

# Contents

## Chapter - IV
## Functions, Modules, Exceptions



## Chapter - V
## Python Error Types



## Chapter - VI
## Exception Handling in Python



## Chapter - VII
## Python Files & Modules

# Preface

*Python is more than just a programming language; it is a gateway to endless possibilities in fields ranging from web development and automation to artificial intelligence and data science. With its simplicity and versatility, Python has become the language of choice for both beginners and seasoned programmers. Hands-On Python Mastery is crafted to guide readers through a practical, step-by-step journey into the world of Python, helping them not only understand the language but also apply it effectively to solve real-world problems.*

*This book is designed to offer a balanced approach, combining theoretical concepts with hands-on practice. Each chapter is filled with carefully structured examples, exercises, and projects that encourage active learning. From foundational programming principles to advanced topics like data visualization and web application development, this book caters to readers of all skill levels. By the end of this journey, readers will have gained the confidence and expertise to tackle a wide array of challenges, turning Python into a powerful tool for innovation and problem-solving.*

**Author**

# CHAPTER I
## Introduction to Python

### 1.1 Definition

- Python is a high-level, object-oriented and interpreted scripting language. It uses English keywords frequently and it has fewer syntactical constructions than other languages.
- Python is Interpreted: Similar to PERL and PHP, python do not require to compile your program before executing the program. Python is processed at runtime by the interpreter.
- Python is Interactive: You can interact with the interpreter directly by sit at a Python prompt and to write your programs.
- Python is Object-Oriented: Python supports Object-Oriented programming that encapsulates code within objects.
- Python is a Beginner's Language: Python is a great language for the beginner-level programmers and supports the development of a wide range of applications from simple text processing to WWW browsers to games.

### 1.2 History of Python

- Python was developed by Guido van Rossum at the National Research Institute for Mathematics and Computer Science in the Netherlands in the late eighties and early nineties.
- Python is derived from many other languages, including ABC, Modula-3, C, C++, Algol-68, SmallTalk, Unix shell, and other scripting languages.
- Python is now maintained by a core development team at the institute, although Guido van Rossum still holds a vital role in directing its progress.
- Python 1.0 was released on 20 February, 1991.

- Python 2.0 was released on 16 October 2000 and had many major new features, including a cycle detecting garbage collector and support for Unicode. With this release the development process was changed and became more transparent and community- backed.
- Python 3.0 (which early in its development was commonly referred to as Python 3000 or py3k), a major, backwards-incompatible release, was released on 3 December 2008 after a long period of testing. Many of its major features have been back ported to the backwards-compatible Python 2.6.x and 2.7.x version series.
- In January 2017 Google announced work on a Python 2.7 to go transcompiler, which The Register speculated was in response to Python 2.7's planned end-of-life.

## 1.3 Python Features

Python's has many features include:

- Easy-to-learn: Python has few keywords, simple structure, and a clearly defined syntax. This allows the student to pick up the language quickly.
- Easy-to-read: Python code is more clearly defined and visible to the eyes.
- Easy-to-maintain: Python's source code is fairly easy-to-maintain.
- A broad standard library: Python's bulk of the library is very portable and cross- platform compatible on UNIX, Windows, and Macintosh.
- Interactive Mode: Python has support for an interactive mode which allows interactive testing and debugging of snippets of code.
- Portable: Python can run on a wide variety of hardware platforms and has the same interface on all platforms.
- Extendable: You can add low-level modules to the Python interpreter. These modules enable programmers to add to or customize their tools to be more efficient.

- Databases: Python provides interfaces to all major commercial databases.
- GUI Programming: Python supports GUI applications that can be created and ported to many system calls, libraries, and windows systems, such as Windows MFC, Macintosh, and the X Window system of UNIX.
- Scalable: Python provides a better structure and support for large programs than shell scripting.

## 1.4 Need of Python Programming

- **Software quality**

Python code is designed to be readable, and hence reusable and maintainable— much more so than traditional scripting languages. The uniformity of Python code makes it easy to understand, even if you did not write it. In addition, Python has deep support for more advanced software reuse mechanisms, such as object-oriented (OO) and function programming.

- **Developer productivity**

Python boosts developer productivity many times beyond compiled or statically typed languages such as C, C++, and Java. Python code is typically one-third to less to debug, and less to maintain after the fact. Python programs also run immediately, without the lengthy compile and link steps required by some other tools, further boosting programmer speed.

- **Program portability**

Most Python programs run unchanged on all major computer platforms. Porting Python code between Linux and Windows, for example, is usually just a matter of copying a script_s code between machines.

- **Support libraries**

Python comes with a large collection of prebuilt and portable functionality, known as the standard library. This library supports an array of application-level programming tasks, from text pattern matching to network scripting. In addition, Python can be extended with both home grown libraries and a vast collection of third-party application support software. Python_s third-party domain offers tools for website construction, numeric programming, serial port access, game development, and much more (see ahead for a sampling).

- **Component integration**

Python scripts can easily communicate with other parts of an application, using a variety of integration mechanisms. Such integrations allow Python to be used as a product customization and extension tool. Today, Python code can invoke C and C++ libraries, can be called from C and C++ programs, can integrate with Java and .NET components, can communicate over frameworks such as COM and Silverlight, can interface with devices over serial ports, and can interact over networks with interfaces like SOAP, XML-RPC, and CORBA. It is not a standalone tool.

- **Enjoyment**

Because of Python_s ease of use and built-in toolset, it can make the act of programming more pleasure than chore. Although this may be an intangible benefit, its effect on productivity is an important asset. Of these factors, the first two (quality and productivity) are probably the most compelling benefits to most Python users, and merit  a fuller description.

- **It's Object-Oriented**

Python is an object-oriented language, from the ground up. Its class model supports advanced notions such as polymorphism, operator overloading, and multiple inheritance; yet in the context of Python's dynamic typing, object-oriented programming (OOP) is remarkably easy to apply. Python's OOP nature makes it ideal as a  scripting tool for object-oriented systems languages such as

C++ and Java. For example, Python programs can subclass (specialized) classes implemented in C++ or Java.

- **It's Free**

Python is freeware—something which has lately been come to be called open source software. As with Tcl and Perl, you can get the entire system for free over the Internet. There are no restrictions on copying it, embedding it in your systems, or shipping it with your products. In fact, you can even sell Python, if you're so inclined. But don't get the wrong idea: "free" doesn't mean "unsupported". On the contrary, the Python online community responds to user queries with a speed that most commercial software vendors would do well to notice.

- **It's Portable**

Python is written in portable ANSI C, and compiles and runs on virtually every major platform in use today. For example, it runs on UNIX systems, Linux, MS-DOS, MS-Windows (95, 98, NT), Macintosh, Amiga, Be-OS, OS/2, VMS, QNX, and more. Further, Python programs are automatically compiled to portable bytecode, which runs the same on any platform with a compatible version of Python installed (more on this in the section "It's easy to use"). What that means is that Python programs that use the core language run the same on UNIX, MS-Windows, and any other system with a Python interpreter.

- **It's Powerful**

From a features perspective, Python is something of a hybrid. Its tool set places it between traditional scripting languages (such as Tcl, Scheme, and Perl), and systems languages (such as C, C++, and Java). Python provides all the simplicity and ease of use of a scripting language, along with more advanced programming tools typically found in systems development languages.

- **Automatic memory management**

Python automatically allocates and reclaims ("garbage collects") objects when no longer used, and most grow and shrink on demand; Python, not you, keeps track of low- level memory details.

- **Programming-in-the-large support**

Finally, for building larger systems, Python includes tools such as modules, classes, and exceptions; they allow you to organize systems into components, do OOP, and handle events gracefully.

- **It's Mixable**

Python programs can be easily "glued" to components written in other languages. In technical terms, by employing the Python/C integration APIs, Python programs can be both extended by (called to) components written in C or C++, and embedded in (called by) C or C++ programs. That means you can add functionality to the Python system as needed and use Python programs within other environments or systems.

- **It's Easy to Use**

For many, Python's combination of rapid turnaround and language simplicity make programming more fun than work. To run a Python program, you simply type it and run it. There are no intermediate compile and link steps (as when using languages such as C or C++). As with other interpreted languages, Python executes programs immediately, which makes for both an interactive programming experience and rapid turnaround after program changes. Strictly speaking, Python programs are compiled (translated) to an intermediate form called bytecode, which is then run by the interpreter.

- **It's Easy to Learn**

This brings us to the topic of this book: compared to other programming languages, the core Python language is amazingly easy to learn. In fact In fact, you can expect to be coding significant Python programs in a matter of days (and perhaps in just hours, if you're already an experienced programmer).

- **Internet Scripting**

Python comes with standard Internet utility modules that allow Python programs to communicate over sockets, extract form information sent to a server-side CGI script, parse HTML, transfer files by FTP, process XML files, and much more. There are also a number of peripheral tools for doing Internet programming in Python. For instance, the HTMLGen and pythondoc systems generate HTML files from Python class-based descriptions, and the JPython system mentioned above provides for seamless Python/Java integration.

- **Database Programming**

Python's standard pickle module provides a simple object-persistence system: it allows programs to easily save and restore entire Python objects to files. For more traditional database demands, there are Python interfaces to Sybase, Oracle, Informix, ODBC, and more. There is even a portable SQL database API for Python that runs the same on a variety of underlying database systems, and a system named gadfly that implements an SQL database for Python programs.

- **Image Processing, AI, Distributed Objects, Etc.**

Python is commonly applied in more domains than can be mentioned here. But in general, many are just instances of Python's component integration role in action. By adding Python as a frontend to libraries of components written in a compiled language such as C, Python becomes useful for scripting in a variety of domains. For instance, image processing for Python is implemented as a set of library components implemented in a compiled language such as C, along with a Python frontend layer on top used to configure and launch the compiled components.

## Who Uses Python Today?

- Google makes extensive use of Python in its web search systems.
- The popular YouTube video sharing service is largely written in Python.
- The Dropbox storage service codes both its server and desktop client software primarily in Python.
- The Raspberry Pi single-board computer promotes Python as its educational language.
- The widespread BitTorrent peer-to-peer file sharing system began its life as a Python program.
- Google_s App Engine web development framework uses Python as an application language.
- Maya, a powerful integrated 3D modeling and animation system, provides a Python scripting API.
- Intel, Cisco, Hewlett-Packard, Seagate, Qualcomm, and IBM use Python for hardware testing.
- NASA, Los Alamos, Fermilab, JPL, and others use Python for scientific programming tasks.

## Byte code Compilation:

Python first compiles your source code (the statements in your file) into a format known as byte code. Compilation is simply a translation step, and byte code  is  a  lower-  level, platform independent representation of your source code. Roughly, Python translates each of your source statements into a group of byte code instructions by decomposing them into individual steps. This byte code translation is performed to speed execution —byte code can be run much more quickly than the original source code statements in your text file.

**The Python Virtual Machine:**

Once your program has been compiled to byte code (or the byte code has been loaded from existing .pyc file), it is shipped off for execution to something generally known as the python virtual machine (PVM).

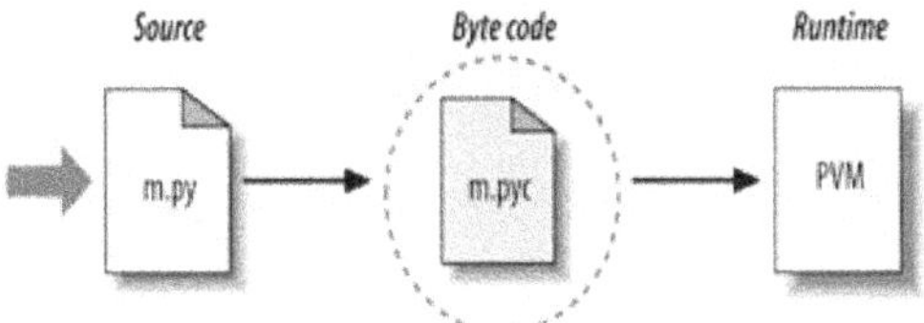


Figure 1. Virtual Machine

## 1.5 Applications of Python

1. Systems Programming
2. GUIs
3. Internet Scripting
4. Component Integration
5. Database Programming
6. Rapid Prototyping
7. Numeric and Scientific Programming

**What Are Python's Technical Strengths?**

1. It_s Object-Oriented and Functional
2. It_s Free
3. It_s Portable
4. It_s Powerful
5. It_s Mixable
6. It_s Relatively Easy to Use
7. It_s Relatively Easy to Learn

## 1.6 Download and installation of Python software

Step 1: Go to website www.python.org and click downloads select version which you want.

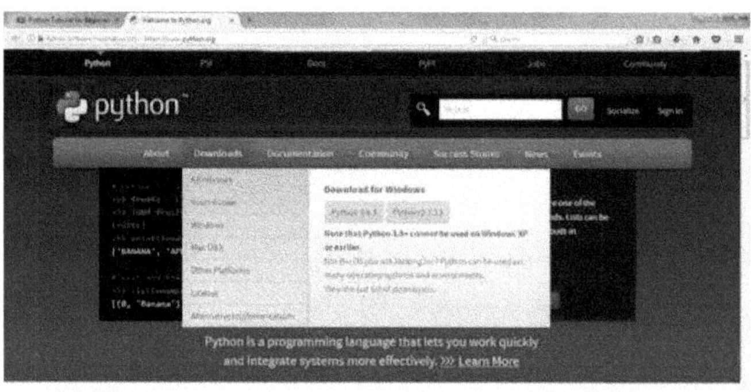

Step 2: Click on Python 2.7.13 and download. After download open the file.

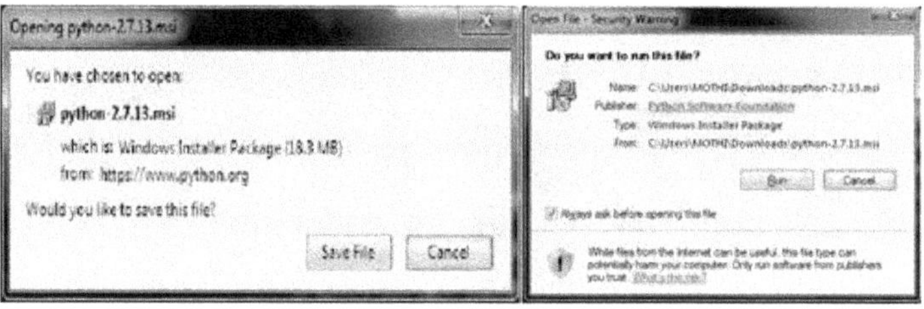

Step 3: Click on Next to continue.

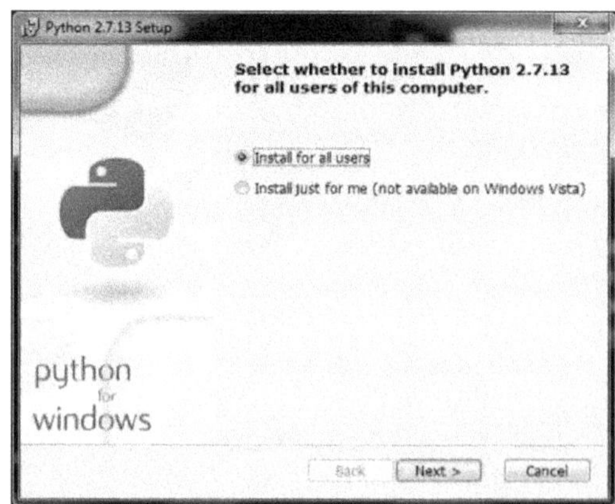

Step 4: After installation location will be displayed. The Default location is C:\Python27.

Click on next to continue.

Step 5: After the python interpreter and libraries are displayed for installation. Click on Next to continue.

Step 6: The installation has been processed.

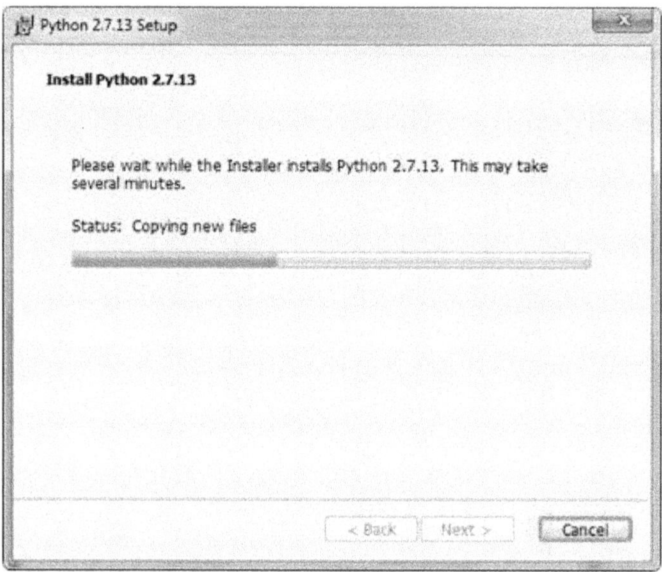

Step 7: Click the Finish to complete the installation.

## 1.7 Setting up PATH to python:

- Programs and other executable files can be in many directories, so operating systems provide a search path that lists the directories that the OS searches for executables.

- The path is stored in an environment variable, which is a named string maintained by the operating system. This variable contains information available to the command shell and other programs.

- Copy the Python installation location C:\Python27

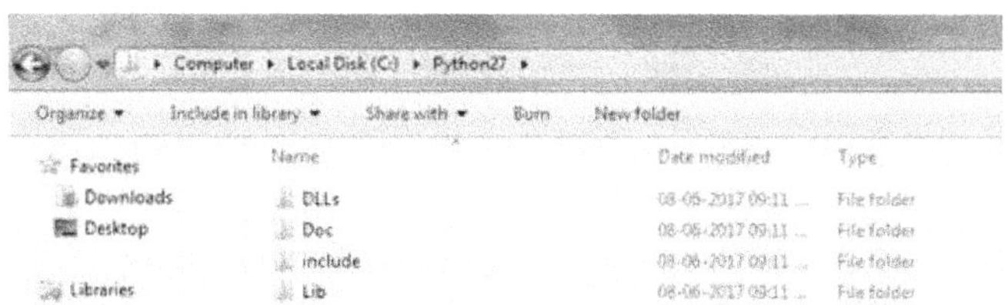

- Right-click the My Computer icon on your desktop and choose Properties. And then select Advanced System properties.

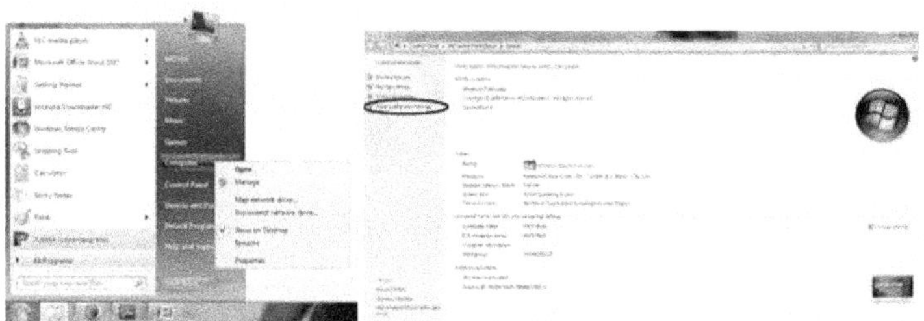

- Goto Environment Variables and go to System Variables select Path and click on Edit.

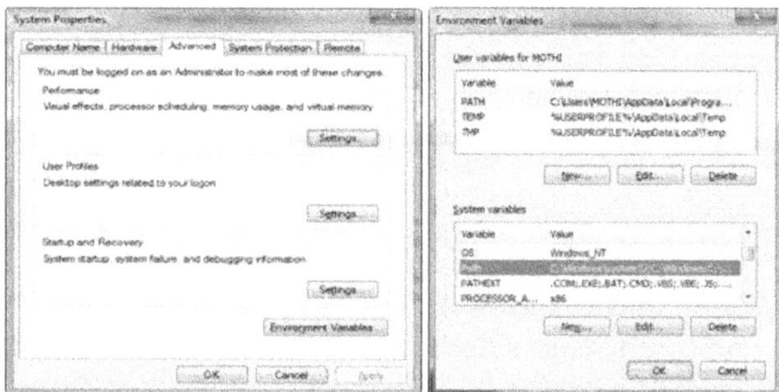

- Add semicolon (;) at end and copy the location C:\Python27 and give semicolon (;) and click OK.

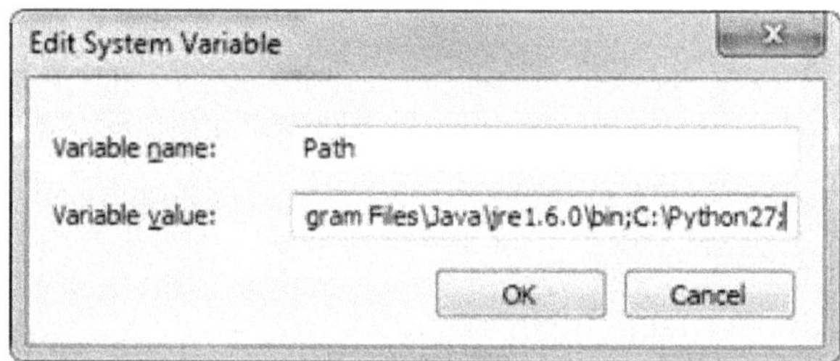

## 1.8 Running Python

a. Running Python Interpreter:

Python comes with an interactive interpreter. When you type python in your shell or command prompt, the python interpreter becomes active with a >>> prompt and waits for your commands.

```
Python 2.7.13 (v2.7.13:a06454b1afa1, Dec 17 2016, 20:42:59) [MSC v.1500 32 bit (Intel)]
on win32
Type "copyright", "credits" or "license()" for more information.
>>>
```

Now you can type any valid python expression at the prompt. Python reads the typed expression, evaluates it and prints the result.

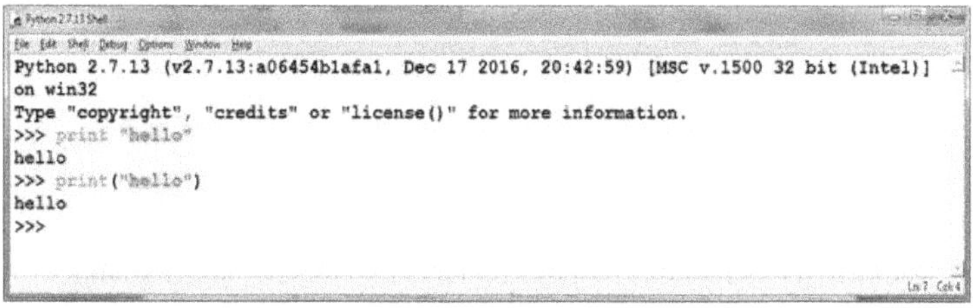

b. Running Python Scripts in IDLE:

- Goto File menu click on New File (CTRL+N) and write the code and save add.py a=input("Enter a value ")
- b=input("Enter b value ") c=a+b
- print "The sum is",c
- And run the program by pressing F5 or RunRun Module.

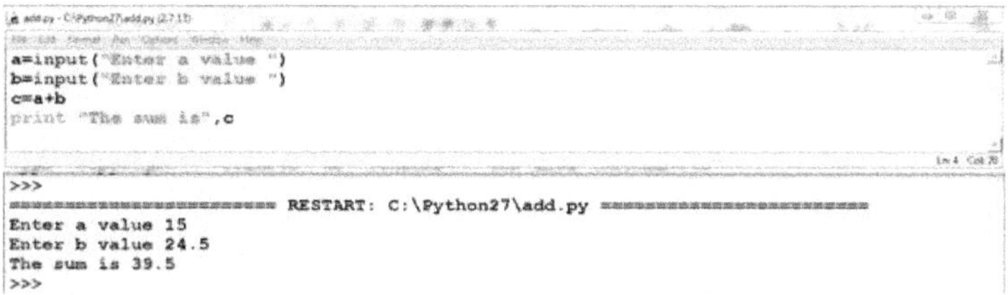

c. Running python scripts in Command Prompt

Before going to run we have to check the PATH in environment variables.

Open your text editor, type the following text and save it as hello.py.

**print "hello"**

And run this program by calling python hello.py. Make sure you change to the directory where you saved the file before doing it.

```
Administrator: Command Prompt

Microsoft Windows [Version 6.1.7601]
Copyright (c) 2009 Microsoft Corporation.  All rights reserved.

C:\Users\MOTHI>python hello.py
hello

C:\Users\MOTHI>
```

## 1.9 Install PyCharm Python IDE in Windows

If you are new to programming then you may be wondering what do we mean by IDE? IDE stands for integrated development environment. It is a software that consolidates the basic tools that are required to write and test programs in a certain language. Typically, an IDE contains a code editor, a compiler or interpreter and a debugger that you can access at the same place through IDE GUI.

1. Go to this link: https://www.jetbrains.com/pycharm/download/ and click

2. Download the community edition.

3. After the files downloaded double click the exe files and follow the default procedures

Install Jupyter Notebook

1. Type this link in the web browser : https://jupyter.org/try

2. Then you will get screen like below:

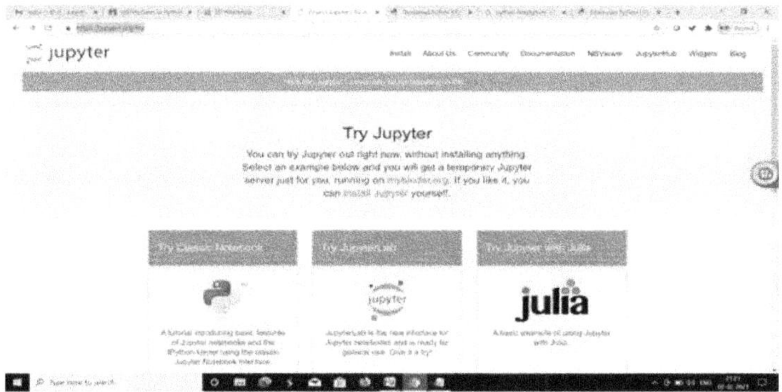

3. Click Try Classic Notebook

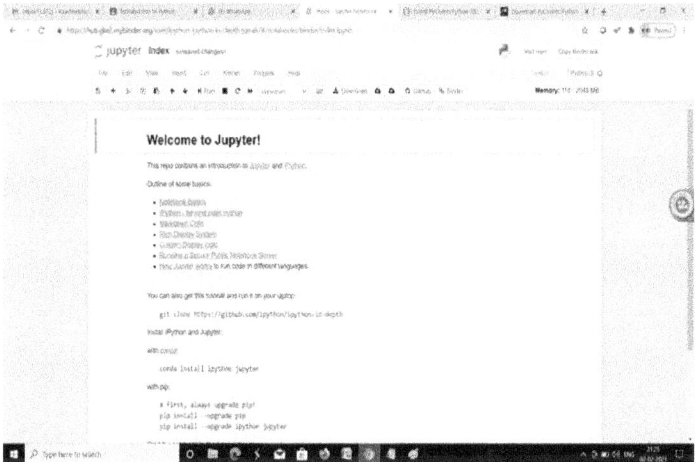

4. Click File ->New Notebook□python3

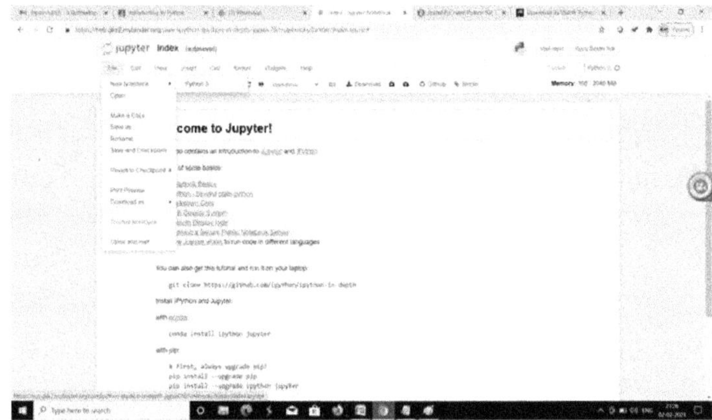

5. Type the programs and click run

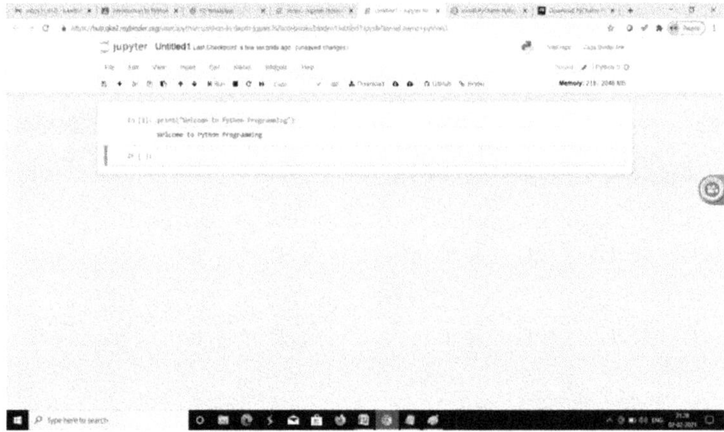

## 2.0 Install Spyder

1. Go to https://www.spyder-ide.org/

2. Read the instructions and proceed with download.

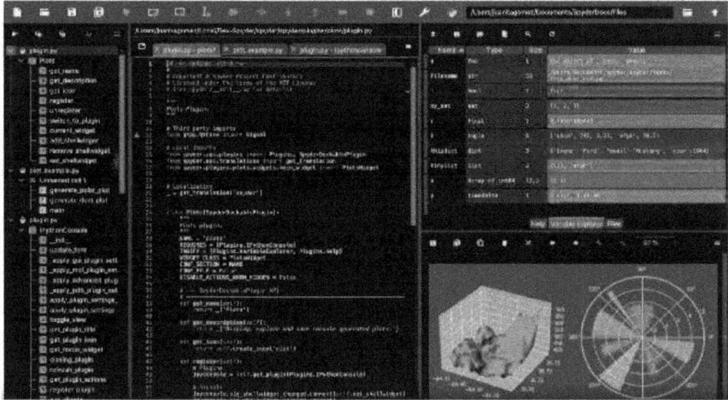

3. Process with the Spider IDE.

Google Colab

Google Colaboratory or Colab is major product from Google Research. It allows anyone to write and execute python code via browser. It is mainly used for machine learning, data anlysis and education purposes. It is hosted by Jupyter notebook service.

Colab does not require any prerequisites to set up. It is free of charge. It also provides free computing resources which also includes GPUs. It is easy to use in terms of coding, computation, sharing and analyzing. It reduces the computation cost when comparing with other IDE's.

# CHAPTER II

# Python Variables, Input Functions And Data Types

Variables are reserved memory locations to store values. This means that when you create a variable you reserve some space in memory. Based on the data type of a variable, the interpreter allocates memory and decides what can be stored in the reserved memory. Therefore, by assigning different data types to variables, you can store integers, decimals or characters in these variables.

## 2.1 Assigning Values to Variables

Python variables do not need explicit declaration to reserve memory space. The declaration happens automatically when you assign a value to a variable. The equal sign (=) is used to assign values to variables. The operand to the left of the = operator is the name of the variable and the operand to the right of the = operator is the value stored in the variable. For example

```
Python 2.7.13 Shell
File  Edit  Shell  Debug  Options  Window  Help
Python 2.7.13 (v2.7.13:a06454b1afa1, Dec 17 2016, 20:42:59) [MSC v.1500 32 bit (Intel)]
on win32
Type "copyright", "credits" or "license()" for more information.
>>> a=20
>>> b=35
>>> c=a+b
>>> print "The sum is ",c
The sum is  55
>>>
```

## Multiple Assignments to variables:

Python allows you to assign a single value to several variables simultaneously. For example –

$$a = b = c = 10$$

Here, an integer object is created with the value 1, and all three variables are assigned to the same memory location. You can also assign multiple objects to multiple variables. For example –

a, b, c = 10, 20," karthee"

Here, two integer objects with values 1 and 2 are assigned to variables a and b respectively, and one string object with the value "karthee" is assigned to the variable c.

## 2.2 Keywords

The following list shows the Python reserved words or keywords. These are reserved words we cannot use them as constant or variable or any other identifier names. All the Python keywords contain lowercase letters only.

| | | | |
|---|---|---|---|
| and | elif | if | print |
| as | else | import | raise |
| assert | except | in | return |
| break | exec | is | try |
| class | finally | lambda | while |
| continue | for | not | with |
| def | from | or | yield |
| del | global | pass | |

## 2.3 INPUT Function

To get input from the user you can use the input function. When the input function is called the program stops running the program, prompts the user to enter something at the keyboard by printing a string called the prompt to the screen, and then waits for the user to press the Enter key. The user types a string of characters and presses enter. Then the input function returns that string and Python continues running the program by executing the next statement after the input statement. Python provides the function input(). input has an optional parameter, which is the prompt string.

For example,

```
name=input("Enter your name ")
print "The name is",name
```

```
======================= RESTART: C:/Python27/name.py =======================
Enter your name "MOTHI"
The name is MOTHI
>>>
```

## 2.4 OUTPUT function

We use the print () function or print keyword to output data to the standard output device (screen). This function prints the object/string written in function. The actual syntax of the print () function is

print(*objects, sep=' ', end='\n', file=sys.stdout, flush=False).

Here, objects is the value(s) to be printed. The sep separator is used between the values. It defaults into a space character. After all values are printed, end is printed. It defaults into a new line ( \n ).

```
Python 2.7.13 (v2.7.13:a06454b1afa1, Dec 17 2016, 20:42:59) [MSC v.1500 32 bit (Intel)]
on win32
Type "copyright", "credits" or "license()" for more information.
>>> print "hello"
hello
>>> print "hello","hai"
hello hai
>>> print "hello"+"hai"
hellohai
>>> print("hello")
hello
>>> print("hello","hai")
('hello', 'hai')
>>> print("hello"+"hai")
hellohai
>>>
```

```
print "WELCOME",
print "To CSE"

>>>
========================= RESTART: C:/Python27/wel.py =========================
WELCOME To CSE
>>>
```

## 2.5 Indentation

Code blocks are identified by indentation rather than using symbols like curly braces. Without extra symbols, programs are easier to read. Also, indentation clearly identifies which block of code a statement belongs to. Of course, code blocks can consist of single statements, too. When one is new to Python, indentation may come as a surprise. Humans generally prefer to avoid change, so perhaps after many years of coding with brace delimitation, the first impression of using pure indentation may not be completely positive. However, recall that two of Python's features are that it is simplistic in nature and easy to read.

Python does not support braces to indicate blocks of code for class and function definitions or flow control. Blocks of code are denoted by line indentation. All the continuous lines indented with same number of spaces would form a block. Python strictly follow indentation rules to indicate the blocks.

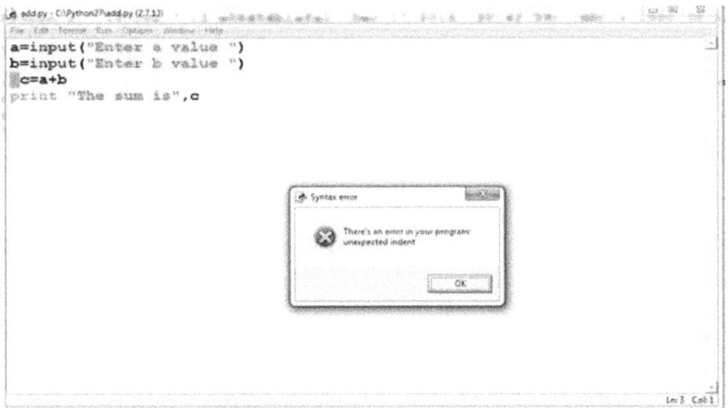



## 2.6 Standard Data Types

The data stored in memory can be of many types. For example, a person's age is stored as a numeric value and his or her address is stored as alphanumeric characters. Python has various standard data types that are used to define the operations possible on them and the storage method for each of them.

**Python has five standard data types:**

- Numbers
- String
- Boolean
- List
- Tuple
- Set
- Dictionary

**Python Numbers:**

Number data types store numeric values. Number objects are created when you assign a value to them.

Python supports four different numerical types:

- int (signed integers)
- long (long integers, they can also be represented in octal and hexadecimal)
- float (floating point real values)
- complex (complex numbers)

Python allows you to use a lowercase L with long, but it is recommended that you use only an uppercase L to avoid confusion with the number 1. Python displays long integers with an uppercase L.

A complex number consists of an ordered pair of real floating-point numbers denoted by x + yj, where x is the real part and b is the imaginary part of the complex number.

**For example:**

Program:

```
a = 3
b = 2.65
c = 98657412345L
d = 2+5j
print "int is",a print "float is",b print "long is",c
print "complex is",d
```

Output:

```
int is 3
float is 2.65
long is 98657412345
complex is (2+5j)
```

## Python Strings

Strings in Python are identified as a contiguous set of characters represented in the quotation marks. Python allows for either pairs of single or double quotes. Subsets of strings can be taken using the slice operator ([ ] and [:] ) with indexes starting at 0 in the beginning of the string and working their way from -1 at the end.

The plus (+) sign is the string concatenation operator and the asterisk (*) is the repetition operator. For example:

Program:

```
str ="WELCOME"
print str # Prints complete string
print str[0] # Prints first character of the string
print str[2:5] # Prints characters starting from 3rd to 5th
print str[2:] # Prints string starting from 3rd character
print str * 2 # Prints string two times
print str + "CSE" # Prints concatenated string
```

Output:

```
WELCOME W
LCO LCOME
WELCOMEWELCOME WELCOMECSE
```

## Built-in String methods for Strings:

| S.No. | Method Name | Descriptions |
|---|---|---|
| 1 | capitalize() | Capitalizes first letter of string. |
| 2 | center(width, fillchar) | Returns a space-padded string with the original string centered to a total of width columns. |
| 3 | count(str,beg= 0,end=len(string) ) | Counts how many times str occurs in string or in a substring of string if starting index beg and ending index end are given. |

| | | |
|---|---|---|
| 4 | decode(encoding ='UTF-8',errors='strict') | Decodes the string using the codec registered for encoding. Encoding defaults to the default string encoding. |
| 5 | encode(encoding ='UTF-8',errors='strict') | Returns encoded string version of string; on error, default is to raise a Value Error unless errors is given with 'ignore' or 'replace'. |
| 6 | endswith(suffix,beg=0, end=len(string)) | Determines if string or a substring of string (if starting index beg and ending index end are given) ends with suffix; returns true if so and false otherwise. |
| 7 | expandtabs(tabsize=8) | Expands tabs in string to multiple spaces; defaults to 8 spaces per tab if tabsize not provided. |
| 8 | find(str,beg=0 end=len(string)) | Determine if str occurs in string or in a substring of string if starting index beg and ending index end are given returns index if found and -1 otherwise. |
| 9 | index(str, beg=0, end=len(string)) | Same as find(), but raises an exception if str not found. |
| 10 | isalnum() | Returns true if string has at least 1 character and all characters are alphanumeric and false otherwise. |
| 11 | isalpha() | Returns true if string has at least 1 character and all characters are alphabetic and false otherwise. |
| 12 | isdigit() | Returns true if string contains only digits and false otherwise. |
| 13 | islower() | Returns true if string has at least 1 cased character and all cased characters are in lowercase and false otherwise. |
| 14 | isnumeric() | Returns true if a unicode string contains only numeric characters and false otherwise. |
| 15 | isspace() | Returns true if string contains only whitespace characters and false otherwise. |

| 16 | istitle() | Returns true if string is properly "titlecased" and false otherwise. |
|---|---|---|
| 17 | isupper() | Returns true if string has at least one cased character and all cased characters are in uppercase and false otherwise. |
| 18 | join(seq) | Merges (concatenates) the string representations of elements in sequence seq into a string, with separator string. |
| 19 | len(string) | Returns the length of the string. |
| 20 | ljust(width[, fillchar]) | Returns a space-padded string with the original string left-justified to a total of width columns. |
| 21 | lower() | Converts all uppercase letters in string to lowercase. |
| 22 | lstrip() | Removes all leading whitespace in string. |
| 23 | maketrans() | Returns a translation table to be used in translates function. |
| 24 | max(str) | Returns the max alphabetical character from the string str. |
| 25 | min(str) | Returns min alphabetical character from the string str. |
| 26 | replace(old, new [, max]) | Replaces all occurrences of old in string with new or at most max occurrences if max given. |
| 27 | rfind(str, beg=0,end=len(string)) | Same as find(), but search backwards in string. |
| 28 | rindex( str, beg=0, end=len(string)) | Same as index(), but search backwards in string. |
| 29 | rjust(width,[, fillchar]) | Returns a space-padded string with the original string right-justified to a total of width columns. |
| 30 | rstrip() | Removes all trailing whitespace of |

| | | string. |
|---|---|---|
| 31 | split(str="", num=string. count(str)) | Splits string according to delimiter str (space if not provided) and returns list of substrings; split into at most num substrings if given. |
| 32 | splitlines ( num=string.count ('\n')) | Splits string at all (or num) NEWLINEs and returns a list of each line with NEWLINEs removed. |
| 33 | startswith(str, beg=0,end=len(st ring)) | Determines if string or a substring of string (if starting index beg and ending index end are given) starts with substring str; returns true if so and false otherwise. |
| 34 | strip([chars]) | Performs both lstrip() and rstrip() on string. |
| 35 | swapcase() | Inverts case for all letters in string. |
| 36 | title() | Returns "titlecased" version of string, that is, all words begin with uppercase and the rest are lowercase. |
| 37 | translate(table, deletechars="") | Translates string according to translation table str(256 chars), removing those in the del string. |
| 38 | upper() | Converts lowercase letters in string to uppercase. |
| 39 | zfill (width) | Returns original string leftpadded with zeros to a total of width characters; intended for numbers, zfill() retains any sign given (less one zero). |
| 40 | isdecimal() | Returns true if a unicode string contains only decimal characters and false otherwise. |

Example:

```
str1="welcome"
print "Capitalize function---",str1.capitalize() print str1.center(15,"*")
print "length is",len(str1)
print "count function---",str1.count('e',0,len(str1))
```

*print "endswith function---",str1.endswith('me',0,len(str1))*
*print "startswith function---",str1.startswith('me',0,len(str1))*
*print "find function---",str1.find('e',0,len(str1))*
*str2="welcome2017"*
*print "isalnum function---",str2.isalnum()*
*print "isalpha function---",str2.isalpha()*
*print "islower function---",str2.islower()*
*print "isupper function---",str2.isupper()*
*str3="welcome"*
*print "lstrip function---",str3.lstrip()*
*str4="77777777cse777777";*
*print "lstrip function---",str4.lstrip('7')*
*print "rstrip function---",str4.rstrip('7') print "strip function---
",str4.strip('7')*
*str5="welcome to java"*
*print "replace function---",str5.replace("java","python")*
Output:

*Capitalize function--- Welcome*
*****welcome**** length is 7*
*count function--- 2 endswith function--- True startswith function-
-- False find function--- 1*
*isalnum function--- True isalpha function--- False*
*islower function--- True isupper function--- False lstrip function-
-- welcome lstrip function--- cse777777*
*rstrip function--- 77777777cse strip function--- cse*
*replace function--- welcome to python*

**Python Boolean**

Booleans are identified by True or False. Example:

Program:

a = True

b = False print a print b

Output

True False

## Data Type Conversion:

Sometimes, you may need to perform conversions between the built-in types. To convert between types, you simply use the type name as a function. For example, it is not possible to perform —2‖+4 since one operand is integer and the other is string type. To perform this we have convert string to integer i.e., *int("2") + 4 = 6*. There are several built-in functions to perform conversion from one data type to another. These functions return a new object representing the converted value.

| Function | Description |
|---|---|
| int(x [,base]) | Converts x to an integer. |
| long(x [,base] ) | Converts x to a long integer. |
| float(x) | Converts x to a floating-point number. |
| complex(real [,imag]) | Creates a complex number. |
| str(x) | Converts object x to a string representation. |
| repr(x) | Converts object x to an expression string. |
| eval(str) | Evaluates a string and returns an object. |
| tuple(s) | Converts s to a tuple. |
| list(s) | Converts s to a list. |
| set(s) | Converts s to a set. |
| dict(d) | Creates a dictionary, d must be a sequence of (key, value) tuples. |
| frozenset(s) | Converts s to a frozen set. |
| chr(x) | Converts an integer to a character. |
| unichr(x) | Converts an integer to a Unicode character. |
| ord(x) | Converts a single character to its integer value. |
| hex(x) | Converts an integer to a hexadecimal string. |
| oct(x) | Converts an integer to an octal string. |

# CHAPTER III

# Python Decision Making Statements

Decision making is the most important aspect of almost all the programming languages. As the name implies, decision making allows us to run a particular block of code for a particular decision. Here, the decisions are made on the validity of the particular conditions. Condition checking is the backbone of decision making.

In python, decision making is performed by the following statements.

| Statement | Description |
|---|---|
| If Statement | The if statement is used to test a specific condition. If the condition is true, a block of code (if-block) will be executed. |
| If - else Statement | The if-else statement is similar to if statement except the fact that, it also provides the block of the code for the false case of the condition to be checked. If the condition provided in the if statement is false, then the else statement will be executed. |
| Nested if Statement | Nested if statements enable us to use if ? else statement inside an outer if statement. |

## 3.1 IF Statement

- The if statement is used to test a particular condition and if the condition is true, it executes a block of code known as if-block.
- The condition of if statement can be any valid logical expression which can be either evaluated to true or false
- For example, you want to print a message on the screen only when a condition is true then you can use if statement to accomplish this in programming. In this guide, we will learn how to use if statements in Python programming with the help of examples.

Flow chart for if statement is given below:

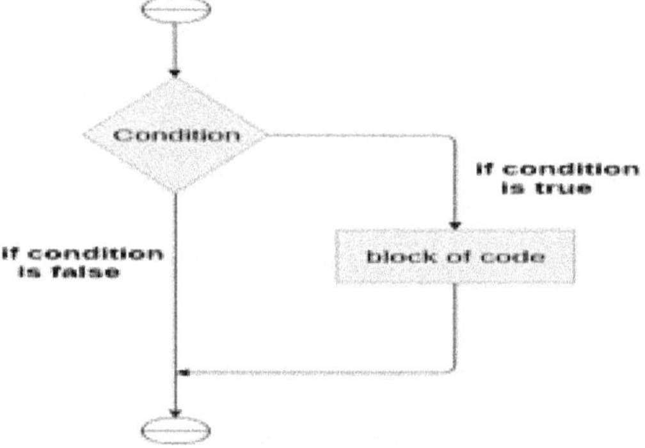


The syntax of the if-statement is given below.

if expression:

    statement

Example:1

```
num = 22
if num % 2 == 0:
    print("Even Number")
```

Example: 2

```
flag = True

if flag==True:

    print("Welcome")

    print("To")

    print ("Dr.K.Kartheeban Python Programming Class")
```

Exmaple:3

```
num = 100
if num < 200:
    print("num is less than 200")
```

## 3.2 If else Statement

- If..else statements are like extension of 'if' statements, with the help of if..else. We can execute certain statements if condition is true and a different set of statements if condition is false.
- For example, you want to print 'even number' if the number is even and 'odd number' if the number is not even, we can accomplish this with the help of if..else statement.

Python – Syntax of if..else statement

```
if condition:
    block_of_code_1
else:
    block_of_code_2
```

If..else flow control

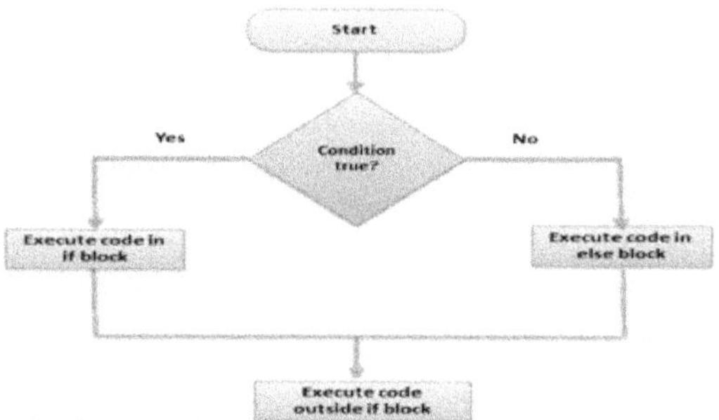


Example 1:

```
num = int(input("Enter the value to find even/odd"))
if num % 2 == 0:
    print("Even Number")
else:
    print("Odd Number")
```

## 3.3 If elif else statement

- The if..elif..else statement is used when we need to check multiple conditions.
- Syntax of if elif else statement in Python

This way we are checking multiple conditions.

*if condition:*
  *block_of_code_1*
*elif condition_2:*
  *block_of_code_2*
*elif condition_3:*
  *block_of_code_3*
  *..*
  *..*
*else:*
  *block_of_code_n*

```python
# menus
print("Calculator")
print("1.Add")
print("2.Substract")
print("3.Multiply")
print("4.Divide")  # input choice
ch=int(input("Enter Choice(1-4): "))
if ch==1:
    a=int(input("Enter A:"))
    b=int(input("Enter B:"))
    c=a+b
    print("Sum = ",c)
elif ch==2:
    a=int(input("Enter A:"))
    b=int(input("Enter B:"))
    c=a-b
    print("Difference = ",c)
elif ch==3:
    a=int(input("Enter A:"))
    b=int(input("Enter B:"))
    c=a*b
    print("Product = ",c)
elif ch==4:
    a=int(input("Enter A:"))
    b=int(input("Enter B:"))
    c=a/b
    print("Quotient = ",c)
else:
    print("Invalid Choice")
```

```
num1 = 10
num2 = 14
num3 = 12
# uncomment following lines to take three numbers from user
#num1 = float(input("Enter first number: "))
#num2 = float(input("Enter second number: "))
#num3 = float(input("Enter third number: "))

if (num1 >= num2) and (num1 >= num3):
   largest = num1
elif (num2 >= num1) and (num2 >= num3):
   largest = num2
else:
   largest = num3

print("The largest number is", largest)
```

When there is an if statement (or if..else or if..elif..else) is present inside another if statement (or if..else or if..elif..else) then this is calling the nesting of control statements.

Syntax of Nested if elif else statement in Python

This way we are checking multiple conditions.

```
if expression1:
    statement(s)
    if expression2:
        statement(s)
    elif expression3:
        statement(s)
    elif expression4:
        statement(s)
    else:
        statement(s)
else:
    statement(s)
```

```
# input three integer numbers
a=int(input("Enter A: "))
b=int(input("Enter B: "))
c=int(input("Enter C: "))

# conditions to find largest
if a>b:
    if a>c:
        g=a
    else:
        g=c
else:
    if b>c:
        g=b
    else:
        g=c
# print the largest number
print("Greater  = ",g)
```

## 3.4 for Loop

A loop is a used for iterating over a set of statements repeatedly. In Python we have three types of loops for, while and do-while. In this guide, we will learn for loop and the other two loops are covered in the separate tutorials.

Syntax of For loop in Python

```
for <variable> in <sequence>:

    # body_of_loop that has set of statements

    # which requires repeated execution
```

Here <variable> is a variable that is used for iterating over a <sequence>. On every iteration it takes the next value from <sequence> until the end of sequence is reached. Lets take few examples of for loop to understand the usage.

Python – For loop example

The following example shows the use of for loop to iterate over a list of numbers. In the body of for loop we are calculating the square of each number present in list and displaying the same.

```
# Program to print squares of all numbers present in a list
# List of integer numbers

numbers = [1, 2, 4, 6, 11, 20]

# variable to store the square of each num temporary

sq = 0

# iterating over the given list
for val in numbers:
    # calculating square of each number
    sq = val * val
    # displaying the squares
    print(sq)
```

**Function range()**

In the above example, we used for loop to iterated over a list. However, range() function also can be used in for loop to iterate over numbers defined by range(). range(n): generates a set of whole numbers starting from 0 to (n-1). For example:

*range(8) is equivalent to [0, 1, 2, 3, 4, 5, 6, 7]*

range(start, stop): generates a set of whole numbers starting from start to stop-1. For example:

*range(5, 9) is equivalent to [5, 6, 7, 8]*

range(start, stop, step_size): The default step_size is 1 which is why when we didn't specify the step_size, the numbers generated are having difference of 1. However by specifying step_size we can generate numbers having the difference of step_size.

For example:

*range(1, 10, 2) is equivalent to [1, 3, 5, 7, 9]*

Lets use the range() function in for loop:

Here we are using range() function to calculate and display the sum of first 5 natural numbers.

Example 1:

```
# Program to print the sum of first 5 natural numbers
# variable to store the sum

sum = 0

# iterating over natural numbers using range()

for val in range(1, 6):
    sum = sum + val      # calculating sum
# displaying sum of first 5 natural numbers
print(sum)
```

Example 2:

```
#Range Controlled Loop

#range(end)  start=0, step=+1
for i in range(10):
    print(i, end=" ")

print("\n")

#range(start, end)  step=+1
for i in range(1, 11):
    print(i, end=" ")

print("\n")

#range(start, end, step)
for i in range(1, 11, 3):
    print(i, end=" ")
print()
for i in range(10, 0, -1):
    print(i, end=" ")
```

Collection Controlled loop

```
#Collection Controlled Loop

names=["karthee", "urmila", "rani", "meena", "dharsini", "kowshik", "kamatchi"]

for item in names:
    print(item)
```

For loop with else block

Unlike java, in Python we can have an optional 'else' block associated with the loop. The 'else' block executes only when the loop has completed all the iterations. Lets take an example:

```
for val in range(5):
        print(val)
else:
        print("The loop has completed execution")
```

Nested For loop in Python

When a for loop is present inside another for loop then it is called a nested for loop. Lets take an example of nested for loop.

```
for i in range(2, 4):
        for j in range(1, 11):
                print(i, "*", j, "=", i*j)
        print()
```

## 3.5 While Loop

While loop is used to iterate over a block of code repeatedly until a given condition returns false. In the last tutorial, we have seen for loop in Python, which is also used for the same purpose. The main difference is that we use while loop when we are not certain of the number of times the loop requires execution, on the other hand when we exactly know how many times we need to run the loop, we use for loop.

*Syntax of while loop*

```
while condition:
    #body_of_while
```

The body_of_while is set of Python statements which require repeated execution. These set of statements execute repeatedly until the given condition returns false.

**Flow of while loop**

1. First the given condition is checked, if the condition returns false, the loop is terminated and the control jumps to the next statement in the program after the loop.

2. If the condition returns true, the set of statements inside loop are executed and then the control jumps to the beginning of the loop for next iteration. These two steps happen repeatedly as long as the condition specified in while loop remains true.

**Python – While loop example**

Here is an example of while loop. In this example, we have a variable num and we are displaying the value of num in a loop, the loop has a increment operation where we are increasing the value of num. This is very important step, the while loop must have a increment or decrement operation, else the loop will run indefinitely, we will cover this later in infinite while loop.

Example 1:

```
num = 1
# loop will repeat itself as long as
# num < 10 remains true

while num < 10:
    print(num)
    #incrementing the value of num
    num = num + 3
```

## Example 2: (Sum of digits of given number)

```python
# Python Program to find Sum of Digits of a Number using While Loop

Number = int(input("Please Enter any Number: "))
Sum = 0

while(Number > 0):
    Reminder = Number % 10
    Sum = Sum + Reminder
    Number = Number // 10

print("\n Sum of the digits of Given Number = %d" %Sum)
```

## Example 3: (Reverse the given number)

```python
# Ask for enter the number from the use

number = int(input("Enter the integer number: "))

# Initiate value to null

revs_number = 0

# reverse the integer number using the while loop

while (number > 0):
    # Logic
    remainder = number % 10
    revs_number = (revs_number * 10) + remainder
    number = number // 10

# Display the result
print("The reverse number is : {}".format(revs_number))
```

## Example 4: (Python Program to Check Armstrong Number)

```python
num = int(input("Enter a number: "))
sum = 0
temp = num

while temp > 0:
    digit = temp % 10
    sum += digit ** 3
    temp //= 10

if num == sum:
    print(num, "is an Armstrong number")
else:
    print(num, "is not an Armstrong number")
```

## 3.6 Break Statement

The break statement is used to terminate the loop when a certain condition is met. We already learned in previous tutorials (for loop and while loop) that a loop is used to iterate a set of statements repeatedly as long as the loop condition returns true. The break statement is generally used inside a loop along with a if statement so that when a particular condition (defined in if statement) returns true, the break statement is encountered and the loop terminates.

For example, lets say we are searching an element in a list, so for that we are running a loop starting from the first element of the list to the last element of the list. Using break statement, we can terminate the loop as soon as the element is found because why run the loop unnecessary till the end of list when our element is found. We can achieve this with the help of break statement (we will see this example programmatically in the example section below).

**Syntax of break statement in Python**

The syntax of break statement in Python is similar to what we have seen in java. In this example, we are searching a number '88' in the given list of numbers. The requirement is to display all the numbers till the number '88' is found and when it is found, terminate the loop and do not display the rest of the numbers.

Example 1:

```
# program to display all the elements before number 88

for num in [11, 9, 88, 10, 90, 3, 19]:
    print(num)
    if(num==88):
            print("The number 88 is found")
            print("Terminating the loop")
            break
Output:
11
9
88
The number 88 is found
Terminating the loop
```

## Python Continue Statement

The continue statement is used inside a loop to skip the rest of the statements in the body of loop for the current iteration and jump to the beginning of the loop for next iteration. The break and continue statements are used to alter the flow of loop, break terminates the loop when a condition is met and continue skip the current iteration.

## Syntax of Continue statement in Python

The syntax of continue statement in Python is similar to what we have seen in Java(except the semicolon)

*continue*

## Example of continue statement

Lets say we have a list of numbers and we want to print only the odd numbers out of that list. We can do this by using continue statement. We are skipping the print statement inside loop by using continue statement when the number is even, this way all the even numbers are skipped and the print statement executed for all the odd numbers.

Example 1:

```
# program to display only odd numbers

for num in [20, 11, 9, 66, 4, 89, 44]:
    # Skipping the iteration when number is even

    if num%2 == 0:
        continue
    # This statement will be skipped for all even numbers
    print(num)
Output:
11
9
89
```

## 3.7 Solved Programs

1. Write a program to Prin the elements in a tuple using while loop

```
KkTuple = (100,200,300,400,500,600)
i = 0

while i < len(KkTuple):
    print(KkTuple[i])
    i += 1
```

2. Write a program to Prin all letters except 'e' and 'r' using Python while loop

```
i = 0
string = "Kartheeban"

#print all letters except 'r' and 'e'

while i < len(string):
    if string[i] == "r" or string[i] == "e":
        i = i + 1
        continue

    print("Result String", string[i])
    i += 1
```

3. Write a program to find the sum of even numbers [ Read input from User]

```
i = 0
sum = 0
n = int(input("Enter the number upto find Even n: "))

while i <= n:
    if i % 2 == 0:
        sum += i
    i += 1

print("Sum of even numbers till n:", sum)
```

4. Write a program to pop all elements from the list.

```python
NameList = ["Kartheeban","K.P.Dharsini","K.P.Kowshik","K.C.Priya"]

while NameList:
    print(NameList.pop())

print(NameList)
```

5. Write a program to display product of the digits of a number received from user.

```python
num=int(input("Enter the number to find product"))
product=1
while(num):
    r=num%10
    product=product*r
    num=num//10
print ("Product of digits is:", product)
```

6. Write a program to print first 10 even numbers in reverse order.

```python
for i in range(20,0,-2):
    print(i)
```

7. Write a program to check if the given number is palindrome or not.

```python
num = int(input("Enter a number: "))
# Input: 232
temp = num
r = 0
while temp > 0:
    rem = temp % 10
    r = (r * 10) + rem
    temp = temp // 10
if num == r:
    print('Given Number is Palindrome:')
else:
    print("Given Number is Not Palindrome:")
```

8. Write a program to generate fibaacci series of a number using while

```
nterms = int(input("How many terms? "))
n1, n2 = 0, 1
count = 0
if nterms <= 0:
    print("Please enter a positive integer")
elif nterms == 1:
    print("Fibonacci sequence upto", nterms, ": ")
    print(n1)
else:
    print("Fibonacci sequence:")
    while count < nterms:
        print(n1)
        nth = n1 + n2
        n1 = n2
        n2 = nth
        count += 1
```

9. Write a program to check wether the given number is prime or not?

```
num = int(input("enter a number: "))
flag = False
if num > 1:
    for i in range(2, num):
        if (num % i) == 0:
            flag = True
            break
if flag:
    print(num, "is not a prime number")
else:
    print(num, "is a prime number")
```

10. Write a program to check the given strin is anagram or not?

```python
def Agram(s1, s2):
    if (sorted(s1) == sorted(s2)):
        print("The strings are anagrams. ")
    else:
        print("The strings aren't anagrams. ")
s1 = input("Enter string1: ")
s2 = input("Enter string2: ")
Agram(s1, s2)
```

11. Write a program to find maximum of two numbers

```python
def maximum(a, b):
    if a >= b:
        return a
    else:
        return b
a = int(input("Enter a number: "))
b = int(input("Enter a number: "))
print(maximum(a, b))
```

12. Write a program to find maximum of three numbers

```python
def maximum(a, b, c):
    if (a >= b) and (a >= c):
        largest = a
    elif (b >= a) and (b >= c):
        largest = b
    else:
        largest = c
    return largest
a = int(input("Enter a number: "))
b = int(input("Enter a number: "))
c = int(input("Enter a number: "))
print(maximum(a, b, c))
```

13. Write a program to fiminimum of two numbers

```
def minimum(a, b):
    if a <= b:
        return a
    else:
        return b
a = int(input("Enter a number: "))
b = int(input("Enter a number: "))
print(minimum(a, b))
```

14. Write a program to finminimum of three numbers

```
def minimum(a, b, c):
    if (a <= b) and (a <= c):
        largest = a
    elif (b <= a) and (b <= c):
        largest = b
    else:
        largest = c
    return largest
a = int(input("Enter a number: "))
b = int(input("Enter a number: "))
c = int(input("Enter a number: "))
print(minimum(a, b, c))
```

# CHAPTER IV

## Functions, Modules, Exceptions

### 4.1 Python Functions

A function is a block of code that contains one or more Python statements and used for performing a specific task.

### Why use function in Python

As I mentioned above, a function is a block of code that performs a specific task. Lets discuss what we can achieve in Python by using functions in our code:

1. Code re-usability: Lets say we are writing an application in Python where we need to perform a specific task in several places of our code, assume that we need to write 10 lines of code to do that specific task. It would be better to write those 10 lines of code in a function and just call the function wherever needed, because writing those 10 lines every time you perform that task is tedious, it would make your code lengthy, less-readable and increase the chances of human errors.

2. Improves Readability: By using functions for frequent tasks you make your code structured and readable. It would be easier for anyone to look at the code and be able to understand the flow and purpose of the code.

3. Avoid redundancy: When you no longer repeat the same lines of code throughout the code and use functions in places of those, you actually avoiding the redundancy that you may have created by not using functions.

## 4.2 Function declaration

*Def function_name(function_parameters):*

    *function_body # Set of Python statements*

    *return # optional return statement*

## 4.3 Calling the function:

*# when function doesn't return anything*

*function_name(parameters)*

OR

*# when function returns something*

*# variable is to store the returned value*

*variable = function_name(parameters)*

Example 1: (Adding two number Using Function)

```
#Python program to add two numbers using function
def add_num(a,b): #function for addition
    sum=a+b;
    return sum; #return value
num1=int(input("input the number 1: "))         #input from user for num1
num2=int(input("input the number 2"))           #input from user for num2
print("The sum is",add_num(num1,num2))               #call te function
```

Output:

input the number one: 34
input the number one: 45
The sum is 79

## Example 2: (Sum of digits of a number Using Function)

```python
# Function to get sum of digits
def getSum(n):
        sum = 0
        # Single line that calculates sum
        while(n > 0):
                sum += int(n % 10)
                n = int(n/10)
        return sum
# Driver code
n = int(input("Enter the number to find Sum of Digits"))
print(getSum(n))

Output
21
```

## Example 3: (Factorial Using Function and for loop)

```python
#Pyton program to find factorial of a number
def factorial(num): #function definition
    fact=1
    for i in range(1, num+1): #for loop for finding factorial
        fact=fact*i
    return fact   #return factorial

number=int(input("Please enter any number to find factorial: "))
result=factorial(number)#function call and assign the value to variable result
print("The factorial of %d = %d"%(number, result))

Please enter any number to find factorial: 6
The factorial of 6 = 720
```

## Example 4: (Factorial  Using Function and while loop)

```python
def factorial(num): #function definition
    fact=1;
    i=1
    while i<=num:
        fact=fact*i
        i=i+1
    return fact

num=input("Enter a number..");
result=factorial(num)
print("factorial of the number: %d" %result)
factorial(num)#function call

Output :
Enter a number..5
factorial of the number: 120
```

## Example 5: (Reverse the number Using Function and while loop)

```python
# Python Program to reverse a number using Functions

def Reverse(Number):   # Function Definition
  rev = 0

  while(Number > 0):
    rem = Number % 10
    rev = (rev * 10) + rem
    Number = Number // 10
    return rev

Number = int(input())
rev = Reverse(Number)  # Function Call
print("%d" % rev)

Output :
Input :
2148
Output:
8421
```

# A simple Python function to check whether x is even or odd

```python
# A simple Python function to check
# whether x is even or odd
def evenOdd(x):
        if (x % 2 == 0):
                print ("even")
        else:
                print( "odd")
# Driver code to call the function
evenOdd(2)
evenOdd(3)
Output
even
odd
```

## 4.4 Pass by Reference or pass by value

Pass by Reference or pass by value

One important thing to note is, in Python every variable name is a reference. When we pass a variable to a function, a new reference to the object is created. Parameter passing in Python is the same as reference passing in Java.

```
# Here x is a new reference to same list lst
def myFun(x):
        x[0] = 20
# Driver Code (Note that lst is modified after function call
lst = [10, 11, 12, 13, 14, 15]
myFun(lst)
print(lst)
Output
[20, 11, 12, 13, 14, 15]
```

When we pass a reference and change the received reference to something else, the connection between the passed and received parameter is broken. For example, consider the below program.

```
def myFun(x):
    # After below line link of x with previous object gets broken. A new object is assigned to x
        x = [20, 30, 40]
# Driver Code (Note that lst is not modified after function call.
lst = [10, 11, 12, 13, 14, 15]
myFun(lst)
print(lst)
Output
[10, 11, 12, 13, 14, 15]
```

Another example to demonstrate that the reference link is broken if we assign a new value (inside the function).

```
def myFun(x):
# After below line link of x with previous object gets broken. A new object is assigned to x.
        x = 20
# Driver Code (Note that lst is not modified after function call.
x = 10
myFun(x)
print(x)
```

Exercise: Try to guess the output of the following code.

```
def swap(x, y):
        temp = x
        x = y
        y = temp
# Driver code
x = 2
y = 3
swap(x, y)
print(x)
print(y)
```

## Default arguments in Function

Now that we know how to declare and call a function, lets see how can we use the default arguments. By using default arguments, we can avoid the errors that may arise while calling a function without passing all the parameters. Lets take an example to understand this:

In this example we have provided the default argument for the second parameter, this default argument would be used when we do not provide the second parameter while calling this function.

Example 1:

```
# default argument for second parameter
def add(num1, num2=1):
    return num1 + num2
sum1 = add(100, 200)
sum2 = add(8)          # used default argument for second param
sum3 = add(100)              # used default argument for second param
print(sum1)
print(sum2)
print(sum3)

Output:
300
9
101
```

```
# Python program to demonstrate default arguments
def myFun(x, y=50):
        print("x: ", x)
        print("y: ", y)
# Driver code (We call myFun() with only argument)
myFun(10)
Output
('x: ', 10)
('y: ', 50)
```

## Keyword arguments

The idea is to allow the caller to specify the argument name with values so that caller does not need to remember the order of parameters.

```
# Python program to demonstrate Keyword Arguments
def student(firstname, lastname):
        print(firstname, lastname)

# Keyword arguments

student(firstname='Kamatchi', lastname='Kartheeban')

student(lastname='Ravi', firstname='kumar')

                        Output
                                ('Kamatchi', 'Kartheeban')
                                ('Kumar', 'Ravi')
```

## Variable-length arguments

We can have both normal and keyword variable number of arguments.

Example 1:

```python
# Python program to illustrate  *args for variable number of arguments
def myFun(*argv):
        for i in argv:
                print(i)
myFun('Hello', 'Welcome', 'to', 'Python Programming')

Output
Hello
Welcome
To
Python Programming
```

Example 2:

```python
# Python program to illustrate *kargs for variable number of keyword arguments
def myFun(**kwargs):
        for key, value in kwargs.items():
                print("%s == %s" % (key, value))
# Driver code
myFun(first='Kamatchi', mid='for', last='Kartheeban')
Output
first == Kamatchi
mid == for
last == Kartheeban
```

Anonymous functions:

In Python, an anonymous function means that a function is without a name. As we already know the def keyword is used to define the normal functions and the lambda keyword is used to create anonymous functions.

```
# Python code to illustrate the cube of a number using lambda
function
def cube(x): return x*x*x
cube_v2 = lambda x : x*x*x
print(cube(7))
print(cube_v2(7))
                                                    Output
                                                      343
                                                      343
```

## 4.5 Types of Functions

There are two types of functions in Python:

1. Built-in functions: These functions are predefined in Python and we need not to declare these functions before calling them. We can freely invoke them as and when needed.

2. User defined functions: The functions which we create in our code are user-defined functions. The add() function that we have created in above examples is a user-defined function.

### First Class functions in Python

A programming language is said to support first-class functions if it treats functions as first-class objects. Python supports the concept of First Class functions. First class objects in a language are handled uniformly throughout. They may be stored in data structures, passed as arguments, or used in control structures.

### Properties of first-class functions:

- A function is an instance of the Object type.
- You can store the function in a variable.
- You can pass the function as a parameter to another function.
- You can return the function from a function.
- You can store them in data structures such as hash tables, lists, …

## Examples illustrating First Class functions in Python

1. Functions are objects: Python functions are first class objects. In the example below, we are assigning function to a variable. This assignment doesn't call the function. It takes the function object referenced by shout and creates a second name pointing to it, karthee.

```python
# Python program to illustrate functions
can be treated as objects


def display(text):
            return text.upper()
print (display('Hello'))
karthee = display
print (karthee('Hello'))

                                    Output
                                    HELLO
```

2. Functions can be passed as arguments to other functions: Because functions are objects we can pass them as arguments to other functions. Functions that can accept other functions as arguments are also called higher-order functions. In the example below, we have created a function greet which takes a function as an argument.

```python
# Python program to illustrate functions can be passed as arguments to other functions
def kupper(text):
            return text.upper()
def klower(text):
            return text.lower()
def greet(func):
            # storing the function in a variable
            greeting =func("""Hi, I am created by a function
            passed as an argument.""")
            print (greeting)


greet(kupper)
greet(klower)
                            Output
            HI, I AM CREATED BY A FUNCTION PASSED AS AN ARGUMENT.
                    hi, i am created by a function passed as an argument.
```

3. Functions can return another function: Because functions are objects we can return a function from another function. In the below example, the create_adder function returns adder function.

```python
# Python program to illustrate functions
# Functions can return another function

def create_adder(x):
        def adder(y):
                return x+y

        return adder

add_15 = create_adder(15)

print (add_15(10))
```

Output:
25

## Python Recursion

A function is said to be a recursive if it calls itself. For example, lets say we have a function abc() and in the body of abc() there is a call to the abc().

## Python example of Recursion

In this example we are defining a user-defined function factorial(). This function finds the factorial of a number by calling itself repeatedly until the base case(We will discuss more about base case later, after this example) is reached.

Example 1: (Factorial of a given number Using Recursion)

```python
# Example of recursion in Python to find the factorial of a given number

def factorial(num):
    """This function calls itself to find
    the factorial of a number"""
    if num == 1:
        return 1
    else:
        return (num * factorial(num - 1))
num = 5
print("Factorial of", num, "is: ", factorial(num))
```

Output:
Factorial of 5 is:  120

## Advantages of recursion

Recursion makes our program:

- Easier to write.
- Readable – Code is easier to read and understand.
- Reduce the lines of code – It takes less lines of code to solve a problem using recursion.

Example Programs Using Functions

Example 1: Find the Max of three numbers

```
def max_of_two( x, y ):
    if x > y:
        return x
    return y

def max_of_three( x, y, z ):
    return max_of_two( x, max_of_two( y, z ) )

print(max_of_three(3, 6, -5))
```

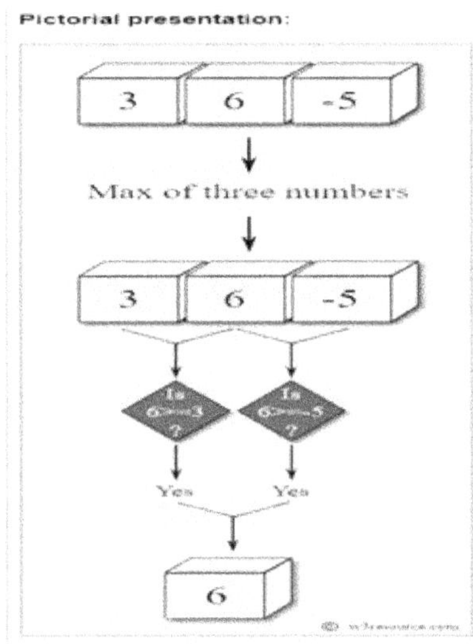

Example 2: Find the sum of all the numbers in a list

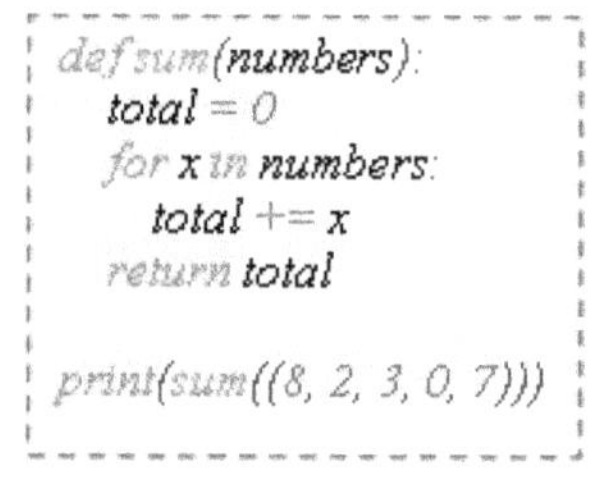


Pictorial presentation:

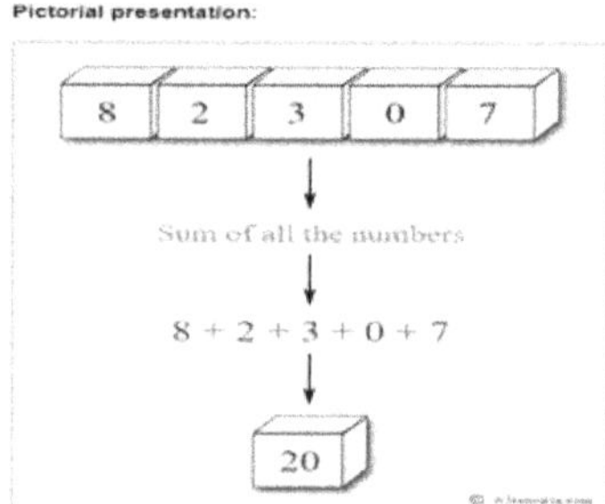


Example 3: Find the multiplication of all the numbers in a list

**Renaming a file**

The python allows you to rename the existing files. The os module helps in file processing operations like renaming, deleting, etc. It also provides rename() method to rename a file to a new name.

Syntax:

*rename(present_name,new_name)*
*Example:*
*import os*
*os.rename("l1.txt"."l2.txt")*

Example 4: Find the factorial of a given number using function using for loop

```python
def factorial(n):
        result = 1
        for i in range(1, n+1):
                result = result*i
        return result


n = int(input('Enter a number: '))
result = factorial(n)
print(n, '! = ', result, sep="")
```

Example 5: Find the factorial of a given number using function using for while

```python
def factorial(n):
        result = 1
        i=1
        while i<=n:
                result*=i
                i+=1
        return result

#read input from user
n = int(input('Enter a number: '))
#calculate factorial
result = factorial(n)
print(result)
```

# CHAPTER V

# Python Error Types

The most common reason of an error in a Python program is when a certain statement is not in accordance with the prescribed usage. Such an error is called a syntax error. The Python interpreter immediately reports it, usually along with the reason.

Errors or inaccuracies in a program are often called as bugs. The process of finding and removing errors is called debugging. Errors can be categorized into three major groups:

- Syntax errors
- Runtime errors
- Logical errors

**5.1 Syntax Errors**

Python will find these kinds of errors when it tries to parse your program, and exit with an error message without running anything. Syntax errors are like spelling or grammar mistakes in a language like English.

**Example: Error Copy**

*>>> print "hello"*

SyntaxError: Missing parentheses in call to 'print'. Did you mean print("hello")?

In Python 3.x, print is a built-in function and requires parentheses. The statement above violates this usage and hence syntax error is displayed.

Many times though, a program results in an error after it is run even if it doesn't have any syntax error. Such an error is a runtime error, called an exception. A number of built-in exceptions are defined in the Python library. Let's see some common error types.

## 5.2 Runtime errors

If a program is free of syntax errors, it will be run by the Python interpreter. However, the program may exit if it encounters a runtime error – a problem that went undetected when the program was parsed, but is only revealed when the code is executed.

- Some examples of Python Runtime errors –
- Division by zero
- Performing an operation on incompatible types
- Using an identifier which has not been defined
- Accessing a list element, dictionary value or object attribute which doesn't exist
- Trying to access a file which doesn't exist

The following table lists important built-in exceptions in Python.

| Exception | Description |
|---|---|
| AssertionError | Raised when the assert statement fails. |
| AttributeError | Raised on the attribute assignment or reference fails. |
| EOFError | Raised when the input() function hits the end-of-file condition. |
| FloatingPointError | Raised when a floating point operation fails. |
| GeneratorExit | Raised when a generator's close() method is called. |
| ImportError | Raised when the imported module is not found. |
| IndexError | Raised when the index of a sequence is out of range. |
| KeyError | Raised when a key is not found in a dictionary. |
| KeyboardInterrupt | Raised when the user hits the interrupt key (Ctrl+c or delete). |
| MemoryError | Raised when an operation runs out of memory. |
| NameError | Raised when a variable is not found in the local or global scope. |
| NotImplementedError | Raised by abstract methods. |

| OSError | Raised when a system operation causes a system-related error. |
|---|---|
| OverflowError | Raised when the result of an arithmetic operation is too large to be represented. |
| ReferenceError | Raised when a weak reference proxy is used to access a garbage collected referent. |
| RuntimeError | Raised when an error does not fall under any other category. |
| StopIteration | Raised by the next() function to indicate that there is no further item to be returned by the iterator. |
| SyntaxError | Raised by the parser when a syntax error is encountered. |
| IndentationError | Raised when there is an incorrect indentation. |
| TabError | Raised when the indentation consists of inconsistent tabs and spaces. |
| SystemError | Raised when the interpreter detects internal error. |
| SystemExit | Raised by the sys.exit() function. |
| TypeError | Raised when a function or operation is applied to an object of an incorrect type. |
| UnboundLocalError | Raised when a reference is made to a local variable in a function or method, but no value has been bound to that variable. |
| UnicodeError | Raised when a Unicode-related encoding or decoding error occurs. |
| UnicodeEncodeError | Raised when a Unicode-related error occurs during encoding. |
| UnicodeDecodeError | Raised when a Unicode-related error occurs during decoding. |
| UnicodeTranslateError | Raised when a Unicode-related error occurs during translation. |
| ValueError | Raised when a function gets an argument of correct type but improper value. |
| ZeroDivisionError | Raised when the second operand of a division or module operation is zero. |

## 5.3 IndexError

The IndexError is thrown when trying to access an item at an invalid index.

Example: IndexError

*>>> L1=[1,2,3]*
*>>> L1[3]*
Traceback (most recent call last):

> *File "<pyshell#18>", line 1, in <module>*

*L1[3]*

IndexError: list index out of range

## 5.4 TypeError

The TypeError is thrown when an operation or function is applied to an object of an inappropriate type.

*>>> '2'+2*

Traceback (most recent call last):

*File "<pyshell#23>", line 1, in <module>*

*'2'+2*

TypeError: must be str, not int

## 5.5 ZeroDivisionError

The ZeroDivisionError is thrown when the second operator in the division is zero.

*>>> x=100/0*

Traceback (most recent call last):

File "<pyshell#8>", line 1, in <module>

x=100/0

# CHAPTER VI

## Exception Handling in Python

Exception handling is a mechanism in Python that allows you to gracefully handle and manage runtime errors or exceptional situations that may occur during the execution of a program. When an error occurs, an exception is raised, and if it is not handled properly, the program may terminate abruptly with an error message. The purpose of exception handling is to catch and handle these exceptions in a controlled manner, allowing your program to recover from errors, provide appropriate error messages, and perform alternative actions. The basic structure of exception handling in Python consists of three keywords: try, except, and optionally finally. Here's an overview of how exception handling works:

The try block: The code that may raise an exception is enclosed within a try block. You place the code that you anticipate might raise an exception inside this block.

The except block: If an exception occurs within the try block, it is caught by an except block that handles the exception. You can have one or more except blocks, each handling a specific type of exception or a general exception.

The finally block (optional): The finally block is executed regardless of whether an exception was raised or not. It is typically used to perform cleanup actions or release resources. Python uses try and except keywords to handle exceptions. Both keywords are followed by indented blocks.

```
try:
    #statements in try block
except:
    #executed when error in try block
```

The following example will throw an exception when we try to devide an integer by a string.

```
try:
    a=5
    b='0'
    print(a/b)
except:
    print('Some error occurred.')
    print("Out of try except blocks.")
```
                                    Output
                              Some error occurred.
                             Out of try except blocks.

As mentioned above, a single try block may have multiple except blocks. The following example uses two except blocks to process two different exception types:

```
try:
    a=5
    b=0
    print (a/b)

except TypeError:
    print('Unsupported operation')

except ZeroDivisionError:
    print ('Division by zero not allowed')
print ('Out of try except blocks')
```
                                    Output
                          Division by zero not allowed
                            Out of try except blocks

## 6.1 else and finally

In Python, keywords else and finally can also be used along with the try and except clauses. When the except block is executed if the exception occurs inside the try block, otherwise the else block gets executed, if the try block is found to be exception free.

```
try:
    #statements in try block
except:
    #executed when error in try block
else:
    #executed if try block is error-free
finally:
    #executed irrespective of exception occured or not
```

The finally block consists of statements which should be executed irrespective of an exception occurring in the try block or not. As a consequence, the error-free try block skips the except clause and enters the finally block before going on to execute the rest of the code. If, however, there's an exception in the try block, the appropriate except block will be processed, and the statements in the finally block will be processed before proceeding to the rest of the code.

The example below accepts two numbers from the user and performs their division. It demonstrates the uses of else and finally blocks.

```
try:
    print('try block')
    x=int(input('Enter a number: '))
    y=int(input('Enter another number: '))
    z=x/y
except ZeroDivisionError:
    print("except ZeroDivisionError block")
    print("Division by 0 not accepted")
else:
    print("else block")
    print("Division = ", z)
finally:
    print("finally block")
    x=0
    y=0
print ("Out of try, except, else and finally blocks.")
```

The first run is a normal case. The out of the else and finally blocks is displayed because the try block is error-free.

Output

```
try block
Enter a number: 10
Enter another number: 2
else block
Division =  5.0
finally block
Out of try, except, else and finally blocks.
```

The second run is a case of division by zero, hence, the except block and the finally block are executed, but the else block is not executed.

Output

> *try block*
> *Enter a number: 10*
> *Enter another number: 0*
> *except ZeroDivisionError block*
> *Division by 0 not accepted*
> *finally block*
> *Out of try, except, else and finally blocks.*

In the third run case, an uncaught exception occurs. The finally block is still executed but the program terminates and does not execute the program after the finally block.

Output

> *try block*
> *Enter a number: 10*
> *Enter another number: xyz*
> *finally block*
> *Traceback (most recent call last):*
> *File "C:\python36\codes\test.py", line 3, in <module>*
> *y=int(input('Enter another number: '))*
> *ValueError: invalid literal for int() with base 10: 'xyz'*

Typically, the finally clause is the ideal place for cleaning up the operations in a process. For example, closing a file irrespective of the errors in read/write operations.

## 6.2 Raise an Exception

Python also provides the raise keyword to be used in the context of exception handling. It causes an exception to be generated explicitly. Built-in errors are raised implicitly. However, a built-in or custom exception can be forced during execution. The following code accepts a number from the user. The try block raises a ValueError exception if the number is outside the allowed range.

```
try:
    x=int(input('Enter a number upto 100: '))
    if x > 100:
        raise ValueError(x)
except ValueError:
    print(x, "is out of allowed range")
else:
    print(x, "is within the allowed range")

Output
Enter a number upto 100: 200
200 is out of allowed range
Enter a number upto 100: 50
50 is within the allowed range
```

## 6.3 Python assert keyword

Assertions in any programming language are the debugging tools which help in smooth flow of code. Assertions are mainly assumptions that a programmer knows always wants to be true and hence puts them in code so that failure of them doesn't allow the code to execute further.

In python assert keyword helps in achieving this task. This statement simply takes input a boolean condition, which when returns true doesn't return anything, but if it is computed to be false, then it raises an AssertionError along with the optional message provided.

Syntax : assert condition, error_message(optional) Parameters:

condition : The boolean condition returning true or false.

error_message : The optional argument to be printed in console in case of AssertionError

Returns : Returns AssertionError, in case the condition evaluates to false along with the error message which when provided.

```
# Python 3 code to demonstrate
# working of assert

# initializing number
a = 4
b = 0
# using assert to check for 0
print ("The value of a / b is : ")
assert b != 0, "Divide by 0 error"

  print (a / b)
```

Output :

The value of a/b is :

**Runtime Exception :**

```
Traceback (most recent call last):
  File  "/home/40545678b342ce3b70beb1224bed345f.py",  line
10, in
assert b != 0, "Divide by 0 error"
AssertionError: Divide by 0 error
```

Example 2:

```
# Python 3 code to demonstrate working of assert Application initializing list of
foods temperatures
batch = [ 40, 26, 39, 30, 25, 21]
# initializing cut temperature
cut = 26
# using assert to check for temperature greater than cut
for i in batch:
        assert i > 26, "Batch is Rejected"
        print (str(i) + " is O.K" )
```

Output :

```
40 is O.K
26 is O.K
39 is O.K
30 is O.K
```

**Runtime Exception :**

Traceback (most recent call last): File
"/home/bd45fb65343814a85b6c19bbe366b419.py", line 13, in
    assert i >= 26, "Batch is Rejected"
AssertionError: Batch is Rejected

# CHAPTER VII

## Python Files & Modules

### 7.1 Working with Files in Python

In Python, a file is a named location on disk to store related information. It is used to permanently store data in a non-volatile memory (e.g., hard drive). Python provides many built-in functions and methods for working with files, allowing you to read data from them, write data into them, and perform various file operations.Similar to other programming language which supports files python also supports file concepts but in very simpler manner like other commends in python.

### Advantages and Disadvantages of Python

Understanding the advantages and disadvantages of using files in Python is crucial for making informed decisions about when and how to leverage file-based storage in your applications. Depending on the use case, other data storage solutions like databases or in-memory data structures may be more suitable.

### Advantages of Using Files in Python

- User Friendly: Python provides very simple mechanisms to handle file operations such as create a file and perform manipulation operations by providing many functions.
- Multiplatform: Python functions will on any platforms such as windows, Unix, Linux and MAC.
- Data Storage: Files enable the storage of large amounts of data, making it possible to handle datasets that might be too large to fit into memory.
- Data Sharing: Files facilitate the sharing of data between different programs or systems. Data saved in a file can be easily transferred and accessed by other applications.

- Configuration and Settings: Files are commonly used to store configuration settings, preferences, or parameters for applications. This allows users to customize the behavior of programs.

**Disadvantages of Using Files in Python:**

- Limited Performance: File operations may have slower performance compared to in-memory data structures. Reading and writing large files can be time-consuming.
- Concurrency Issues: Concurrent access to a file by multiple processes can lead to conflicts and data corruption. Synchronization mechanisms are required to address concurrency issues.
- Security Risks: Files can pose security risks, especially if sensitive information is stored in plaintext. Encryption and proper access controls are necessary to mitigate security concerns.
- File Management Overhead: Managing a large number of files can result in overhead, making file-based storage less efficient for certain scenarios.
- Limited Querying: Unlike databases, files do not support sophisticated querying and indexing. Retrieving specific data from a file may require sequential scanning.
- Platform Dependency: File paths and file systems can vary across platforms, leading to potential issues when dealing with file paths and directory structures in a cross-platform application.
- Storage Space: Storing large datasets in files can consume significant storage space. In situations where storage is a concern, alternative storage solutions may be preferred.
- Versioning Challenges: Managing multiple versions of a file, especially in collaborative environments,

can be challenging. Version control systems are often necessary to address this issue.

## 7.2 Operations on Files in Python

There are many operations are performed in with files in python. We discuss each operation with small examples in the following sections.

### *i. Opening a File:*

The open() function is used to open a file. It requires the file name and the mode in which the file should be opened (read, write, append, etc.).

### *Modes of Opening a File:*

'r': Read (default mode) Opens the file for reading.

'w': Write. Opens the file for writing. Creates a new file or truncates the existing file to zero length.

'a': Append. Opens the file for writing. Creates a new file or appends to the existing file.

'b': Binary mode. Used for non-text files (e.g., images, videos).

'x': Exclusive creation. Creates a new file but fails if the file already exists.

### *ii. Reading from a File*

There are many functions available to perform read operations from the files such as read(), readline(), or readlines() to read data from a file.

### *read()*

The read() method is used to read the entire content of the file.

It returns a string containing the contents of the file.

with open('filename.txt', 'r') )as file:

> *content = file.read()*
> *print(Content)*

readline()- The readline() method reads a single line from the file. Each time you call readline(), it reads the next line in the file.

with open('filename.txt', 'r') as file:

> *line1 = file.readline()*
> *line2 = file.readline()*
> *print("Line 1:", line1)*
> *print("Line 2:", line2)*

readlines()

The readlines() method reads all lines from the file and returns them as a list of strings.Each string in the list represents a line from the file.

with open('filename.txt', 'r') as file:

> *lines = file.readlines()*
> *for line in lines:*
> *print(line)*

readlines() method is useful for large files.

### iii.  Write to an Existing File

Inorder to  write to an existing file, we must add a parameter to the open() function:

"a" - Append - will append to the end of the file

"w" - Write - will overwrite any existing content

**Example**

Open the file "file1.txt" and append content to the file:

f = open("file1.txt", "a")

f.write("Now the file has more content!")

f.close() #open and read the file after the appending:

f = open("file1.txt", "r")

 print (f.read())

### iv.  Delete Folder

To delete an entire folder, use the os.rmdir() method:

Example

> *Remove the folder "myfolder":*
> *import os os.rmdir("myfolder")*

### v. Delete a file

To delete a file, you must import the OS module, and run its os.remove() function:

Example

Remove the file "file.txt":

import os os.remove("file.txt")

### vi. Renaming a file

To rename a file, you must use os.rename() function as below:

Example:

> *rename(present_name,new_name)*

Example:

> *import os*
> *os.rename("l1.txt". "l2.txt")*

What is a Module?

Consider a module to be the same as a code library. A file containing a set of functions you want to include in your application.

## 7.3 Python Math

Python has a set of built-in math functions, including an extensive math module that allows you to perform mathematical tasks on numbers.

### *Built-in Math Functions*

The min() and max() functions can be used to find the lowest or highest value in an iterable:

```python
x = min(5, 10, 25)
y = max(5, 10, 25)

print(x)
print(y)
```

The abs() function returns the absolute (positive) value of the specified number:

```python
x = abs(-7.25)
print(x)
```

The pow(x, y) function returns the value of x to the power of y (xy).

```python
x = pow(4, 3)
print(x)
```

## 7.4 The Math Module

The math module in Python is a built-in module that provides various mathematical operations and functions. It provides a range of mathematical functions for performing common mathematical calculations. Here are some of the commonly used functions and constants available in the math module:

## Mathematical Constants

math.pi -Returns the mathematical constant pi (3.14159...).

math.e  -Returns the mathematical constant e (2.71828...).

## Trigonometric Functions

math.sin(x) - Returns the sine of x, where x is in radians.

math.cos(x) - Returns the cosine of x, where x is in radians.

math.tan(x) - Returns the tangent of x, where x is in radians.

math.asin(x)  - Returns the arcsine of x in radians.

math.acos(x) - Returns the arccosine of x in radians.

math.atan(x) - Returns the arctangent of x in radians.

math.degrees(x)- Converts angle x from radians to degrees.

math.radians(x) - Converts angle x from degrees to radians.

## Exponential and Logarithmic Functions:

math.exp(x) - Returns e raised to the power x.

math.log(x) - Returns the natural logarithm (base e) of x.

math.log10(x) - Returns the base-10 logarithm of x.

math.log2(x) - Returns the base-2 logarithm of x.

## Power and Square Root Functions:

math.pow(x, y) - Returns x raised to the power y.

math.sqrt(x) - Returns the square root of x.

## Other Mathematical Functions:

math.ceil(x) - Returns the smallest integer greater than or equal to x.

math.floor(x) -  Returns the largest integer less than or equal to x.

math.factorial(x) - Returns the factorial of x.

math.gcd(x, y)  - Returns the greatest common divisor of x and y.

math.isqrt(x) -   Returns the integer square root of x.

math.modf(x) -  Returns the fractional and integer parts of x as a tuple.

These are just a few examples of the functions available in the math module. To use these functions, you need to import the math module at the beginning of your Python script or interactive session using the import math statement. Once imported, you can call the functions by prefixing them with math.

For example:

```
import math
radius = 5
area = math.pi * math.pow(radius, 2)
print("Area of the circle:", area)
angle = math.radians(90)
sine_value = math.sin(angle)
print("Sine of 90 degrees:", sine_value)
```

This program calculates the area of a circle using the math.pi constant and computes the sine of a 45-degree angle using the math.radians() and math.sin() functions.  The math.sqrt() method for example, returns the square root of a number:

```
import math
x = math.sqrt(64)
print(x)
```

The math.ceil() method rounds a number upwards to its nearest integer, and the math.floor() method rounds a number downwards to its nearest integer, and returns the result:

```
import math
x = math.ceil(1.4)
y = math.floor(1.4)
print(x) #returns 2
print(y) #returns 1
```

The math.pi constant, returns the value of PI (3.14...):

```
import math
x = math.pi
print(x)
```

## Create a Module

To create a module just save the code you want in a file with the file extension .py:

Example

Save this code in a file named mymodule.py

```
def greeting(name):
    print("Hello, " + name)
```

## Use a Module

Now we can use the module just created, by using the import statement:

Example :

Import the module named mymodule, and call the greeting function:

```
import mymodule
mymodule.greeting("Kartheeban")
```

## Variables in Module

The module can contain functions, as already described, but also variables of all types (arrays, dictionaries, objects etc):

Example

Save this code in the file mymodule.py

```
person1={
  "name": "Kartheeban",
  "age": 26,
  "country": "India"
}
```

Example

Import the module named mymodule, and access the person1 dictionary:

```
import mymodule
a = mymodule.person1 ["age"]
print(a)
```

## Naming a Module

You can name the module file whatever you like, but it must have the file extension .py

Re-naming a Module

You can create an alias when you import a module, by using the as keyword:

Example

Create an alias for mymodule called mx:

```
import mymodule as mx
a = mx.person1 ["age"]
print(a)
```

Built-in Modules

There are several built-in modules in Python, which you can import whenever you like.

Example :

Import and use the platform module:

```
import platform

x = platform.system()
print(x)
```

## Using the dir() Function

There is a built-in function to list all the function names (or variable names) in a module. The dir() function:

Example

List all the defined names belonging to the platform module:

```
import platform
x = dir(platform)
print(x)
```

## Import From Module

You can choose to import only parts from a module, by using the from keyword.

Example

The module named mymodule has one function and one dictionary:

```
def greeting(name):
  print("Hello, " + name)
person1 = {
            "name": "John",
            "age": 36,
            "country": "India"
}
```

Example – Import only the person1 dictionary from the module:

```
from mymodule import person1
print (person1["age"])
```

# CHAPTER VIII

# NumPy

## 8.1 Introduction:

NumPy is a Python library used to work with arrays. NumPy was created in 2005 by Travis Oliphant. It is an open-source project and you can use it freely. NumPy stands for Numerical Python. It also has functions for working in domain of linear algebra, fourier transform, and matrices.

### Why Use NumPy

In Python we have lists that serve the purpose of arrays, but they are slow to process. NumPy aims to provide an array object that is up to 50x time faster than traditional Python lists. The array object in NumPy is called ndarray, it provides a lot of supporting functions that make working with ndarray very easy. Arrays are very frequently used in data science, where speed and resources are very important.

### NumPy Creating Arrays - Create a NumPy nd-array Object

NumPy is used to work with arrays. The array object in NumPy is called ndarray. We can create a NumPy ndarray object by using the array() function.

Example 1:

```
import numpy as np
arr = np.array([1, 2, 3, 4, 5])
print(arr)
print(type(arr))
```

type(): This built-in Python function tells us the type of the object passed to it. Like in above code it shows that arr is numpy.ndarray type. To create an ndarray, we can pass a list, tuple or any array-like object into the array() method, and it will be converted into an ndarray:

Example 2:  Use a tuple to create a NumPy array:

```
import numpy as np
arr = np.array((1, 2, 3, 4, 5))
print(arr)
```

## 0-D Arrays

0-D arrays, or Scalars, are the elements in an array. Each value in an array is a 0-D array.

Example 2:  Creating a 0-D array with value 42:

```
import numpy as np
arr = np.array(42)
print(arr)
```

## 1-D Arrays

An array that has 0-D arrays as its elements is called uni-dimensional or 1-D array. These are the most common and basic arrays. Create a 1-D array containing the values 1,2,3,4,5:

```
import numpy as np
arr = np.array([1, 2, 3, 4, 5])
print(arr)
```

## 2-D Arrays

An array that has 1-D arrays as its elements is called a 2-D array. These are often used to represent matrix or 2nd order tensors.

Example

Create a 2-D array containing two arrays with the values 1,2,3 and 4,5,6:

```
import numpy as np
arr = np.array([[1, 2, 3], [4, 5, 6]])
print(arr)
```

## 3-D arrays

An array that has 2-D arrays (matrices) as its elements is called 3-D array.

These are often used to represent a 3rd order tensor.

Create a 3-D array with two 2-D arrays, both containing two arrays with the values 1,2,3 and 4,5,6:

```
import numpy as np
arr = np.array([[[1, 2, 3], [4, 5, 6]], [[1, 2, 3], [4, 5, 6]]])
print(arr)
```

## Check Number of Dimensions?

NumPy Arrays provides the ndim attribute that returns an integer that tells us how many dimensions the array have.

Example

Check how many dimensions the arrays have:

```
import numpy as np

a = np.array(42)
b = np.array([1, 2, 3, 4, 5])
c = np.array([[1, 2, 3], [4, 5, 6]])
d = np.array([[[1, 2, 3], [4, 5, 6]], [[1, 2, 3], [4, 5, 6]]])
print(a.ndim)
print(b.ndim)
print(c.ndim)
print(d.ndim)
```

## Higher Dimensional Arrays

An array can have any number of dimensions. When the array is created, you can define the number of dimensions by using the ndmin argument.

Example

Create an array with 5 dimensions and verify that it has 5 dimensions:

```
import numpy as np
arr = np.array([1, 2, 3, 4], ndmin=5)
print(arr)
print('number of dimensions :', arr.ndim)
```

## 8.2 NumPy Array Indexing

### Access Array Elements

Array indexing is the same as accessing an array element. You can access an array element by referring to its index number. The indexes in NumPy arrays start with 0, meaning that the first element has index 0, and the second has index 1 etc.

Get the first element from the following array:

```
import numpy as np
arr = np.array([1, 2, 3, 4])
print(arr[0])
```

Get the second element from the following array.

```
import numpy as np
arr = np.array([1, 2, 3, 4])
print(arr[1])
```

Get third and fourth elements from the following array and add them.

```
import numpy as np
arr = np.array([1, 2, 3, 4])
print(arr[2] + arr[3])
```

## Access 2-D Arrays

To access elements from 2-D arrays we can use comma separated integers representing the dimension and the index of the element.

Example

Access the 2nd element on 1st dim:

```
import numpy as np
arr = np.array([[1,2,3,4,5], [6,7,8,9,10]])
print('2nd element on 1st dim: ', arr[0, 1])
```

Example : Access the 5th element on 2nd dim:

```
import numpy as np
arr = np.array([[1,2,3,4,5], [6,7,8,9,10]])
print('5th element on 2nd dim: ', arr[1, 4])
```

## 8.3 NumPy Array Slicing

### Slicing arrays

Slicing in python means taking elements from one given index to another given index.

- We pass slice instead of index like this: [start:end].
- We can also define the step, like this: [start:end:step].
- If we don't pass start its considered 0
- If we don't pass end its considered length of array in that dimension
- If we don't pass step its considered 1

## Example

Slice elements from index 1 to index 5 from the following array:

```
import numpy as np
arr = np.array([1, 2, 3, 4, 5, 6, 7])
print(arr[1:5])
```

Example

Slice elements from index 4 to the end of the array:

```
import numpy as np
arr = np.array([1, 2, 3, 4, 5, 6, 7])
print(arr[4:])
```

Example

Slice elements from the beginning to index 4 (not included):

```
import numpy as np
arr = np.array([1, 2, 3, 4, 5, 6, 7])
print(arr[:4])
```

**Negative Slicing**

Use the minus operator to refer to an index from the end:

Example

Slice from the index 3 from the end to index 1 from the end:

```
import numpy as np
arr = np.array([1, 2, 3, 4, 5, 6, 7])
print(arr[-3:-1])
```

STEP

Use the step value to determine the step of the slicing:

Example

Return every other element from index 1 to index 5:

```
import numpy as np
arr = np.array([1, 2, 3, 4, 5, 6, 7])
print(arr[1:5:2])
```

Example

Return every other element from the entire array:

> *import numpy as np*
> *arr = np.array([1, 2, 3, 4, 5, 6, 7])*
> *print(arr[::2])*

## 8.4 NumPy - Built-in Functions

Generally, numpy has several buil-in functions for performing various operations. The following is the various built-in functions available in python.

### Array Creation:

| | | |
|---|---|---|
| np.array() | - | Create an array from a Python list or tuple. |
| np.zeros() | - | Create an array filled with zeros. |
| np.ones() | - | Create an array filled with ones. |
| np.empty() | - | Create an empty array (uninitialized values). |
| np.arange() | - | Create an array with regularly spaced values. |
| np.linspace() | - | Create an array with evenly spaced values. |
| np.eye() | - | Create a 2D identity matrix. |

### Array Manipulation:

| | | |
|---|---|---|
| **np.reshape()** | - | Reshape an array into a specified shape. |
| **np.concatenate()** | - | Join arrays along a specified axis. |
| **np.split()** | - | Split an array into multiple sub-arrays. |
| **np.transpose()** | - | Permute the dimensions of an array. |
| **np.flatten()** | - | Flatten an array into a 1D array. |
| **np.resize()** | - | Resize an array to a specified shape. |
| **np.append()** | - | Append values to the end of an array. |

The reshape() function in NumPy allows you to change the shape (dimensions) of an array without modifying its data. It returns a new array with the specified shape, while the original array remains unchanged. The reshape() function can be used in various ways to transform the shape of an array. Here are some common use cases:

Example:

1. Reshape 1D array to a 2D array:

```python
import numpy as np
arr = np.array([1, 2, 3, 4, 5, 6])
reshaped_arr = np.reshape(arr, (2, 3))
print(reshaped_arr)
```

Output: [[1 2 3] [4 5 6]]. In this example, the 1D array [1, 2, 3, 4, 5, 6] is reshaped into a 2D array with dimensions (2, 3). The resulting array has two rows and three columns

2. Reshape an array with unknown dimensions:

```python
import numpy as np
arr = np.array([1, 2, 3, 4, 5, 6])
reshaped_arr = np.reshape(arr, (2, -1))
print(reshaped_arr)
```

Output:  [[1 2 3]  [4 5 6]] . In this example, the -1 in the reshape function is used as a placeholder for an unknown dimension. NumPy automatically calculates the appropriate size to fill in for the unknown dimension. In this case, since the original array has 6 elements and we want 2 rows, NumPy determines that there should be 3 columns to fulfill the reshape request.

**Reshape a 2D array to a 1D array:**

```python
import numpy as np
arr = np.array([1, 2, 3, 4, 5, 6])
reshaped_arr = np.reshape(arr, (2, 3, 1))
print(reshaped_arr)
```

Output: [1 2 3 4 5 6]. In this example, the 2D array [[1, 2, 3], [4, 5, 6]] is reshaped into a 1D array. The resulting array contains all the elements of the original array in a single dimension.

Reshape an array to a higher-dimensional array:

```
np.add(), np.subtract(), np.multiply(), np.divide() - Perform element-wise arithmetic operations.
np.sum(), np.mean(), np.median() - Compute the sum, mean, median of array elements.
np.min(), np.max(), np.argmin(), np.argmax(): Find minimum, maximum, and their indices.
np.sqrt(), np.exp(), np.log(), np.sin(), np.cos(): Apply mathematical functions element-wise.
np.dot(), np.matmul(): Perform matrix multiplication.
np.linalg.inv(), np.linalg.det(): Compute the inverse and determinant of a matrix.
np.sort(), np.argsort(): Sort an array and return the sorted indices.
```

Output: [[[1] [2] [3]] [[4] [5][6]]]. In this example, the 1D array [1, 2, 3, 4, 5, 6] is reshaped into a 3D array with dimensions (2, 3, 1). The resulting array has two blocks, each with three rows and one column.

Example:

```python
# Python code to demonstrate matrix operations #add (), #subtract ()
and #divide (). Need to #importing numpy for matrix operations

import numpy

# initializing matrices

x = numpy.array([[11, 22], [44, 55]])

y = numpy.array([[77, 88], [99, 100]])

print ("The element wise addition of matrix is : ")

print (numpy.add(x, y)

print ("The element wise subtraction of matrix is : ")

print (numpy.subtract(x, y))

print ("The element wise division of matrix is : ")

print (numpy.divide(x, y))
```

```
import numpy
# initializing matrices
x = numpy.array([[11, 22], [44, 55]])
y = numpy.array([[77, 88], [99, 100]])
print ("The element wise multiplication of matrix is : ")
print (numpy.multiply(x, y))
print ("The product of matrices is : ")
print (numpy.dot(x, y))
```

## Python code to demonstrate matrix operations   sqrt(), sum() and "Transpose"

```
import numpy
x = numpy.array([[11, 22], [44, 55]])     # initializing matrices
y = numpy.array([[77, 88], [99, 100]])
print ("The element wise square root is : ")  # using sqrt() to print the square root of matrix
print (numpy.sqrt(x))
print ("The summation of all matrix element is : ")
print (numpy.sum(y))

print ("The column wise summation of all matrix is : ")
print (numpy.sum(y, axis=0))

print ("The row wise summation of all matrix is : ")
print (numpy.sum(y, axis=1))

print ("The transpose of given matrix is : ")
print (x.T)
```

## Random Number Generation:

```
np.random.rand()     -       Generate random numbers from a uniform distribution.

np.random.randn()    -        Generate random numbers from a standard normal distribution.

np.random.randint()  -       Generate random integers.

np.random.shuffle()  -       Shuffle the elements of an array.
```

## Generating Random Numbers

```
import numpy as np
random_numbers = np.random.randint(1, 10, size=7)
print("Random numbers:", random_numbers)
```

Statistics and Probability:

```
np.histogram()  - Compute the histogram of an array.

np.mean(), np.median(), np.var(), np.std() - Compute statistical measures.

np.percentile()  - Compute the value below which a given percentage of data falls.
```

These are just some examples of the many built-in functions available in NumPy. The library provides a wide range of functions for array manipulation, mathematical operations, random number generation, statistics, and more, making it a powerful tool for scientific computing and data analysis.

## 8.5 Applications of Numpy

NumPy is a versatile library that is widely used in various domains for numerical computing and data analysis. Here are some applications of NumPy:

**Numerical Computing:** NumPy provides efficient numerical operations on multi-dimensional arrays, making it a fundamental library for scientific computing tasks. It is extensively used in fields such as physics, engineering, and mathematics for tasks like matrix operations, solving linear equations, numerical integration, interpolation, and optimization.

**Data Analysis and Manipulation:** NumPy provides powerful tools for data manipulation, filtering, and analysis. It enables efficient processing of large datasets, as well as the ability to perform complex operations on arrays, such as indexing, slicing, sorting, and reshaping. NumPy arrays also serve as the foundation for many other libraries in the Python ecosystem, such as pandas for data analysis and scikit-learn for machine learning.

**Machine Learning:** NumPy is an integral part of machine learning workflows. It is used for tasks such as data preprocessing, feature extraction, and model evaluation. NumPy arrays efficiently store and process the input data and model parameters, allowing for efficient computation in machine learning algorithms. Many machine learning libraries, including scikit-learn and TensorFlow, rely on NumPy for efficient array operations.

**Image and Signal Processing:** NumPy provides essential tools for image and signal processing tasks. Images and signals can be represented as multi-dimensional arrays, and NumPy enables various operations such as filtering, convolution, Fourier transforms, and statistical analysis on these arrays. Libraries like OpenCV and SciPy often use NumPy arrays as the data format for image and signal processing tasks.

**Simulation and Modeling:** NumPy is used for numerical simulations and modeling in scientific research and engineering. It allows for efficient implementation of mathematical models and simulations, enabling researchers to study complex systems, perform Monte Carlo simulations, solve differential equations, and analyze simulation results.

**Financial and Economic Analysis:** NumPy provides tools for financial and economic analysis, allowing for efficient computation and analysis of financial data. It supports tasks such as time series analysis, portfolio optimization, risk assessment, and statistical modeling. Libraries like pandas and statsmodels build on top of NumPy to provide higher-level functionalities for financial analysis.

These are just a few examples of the diverse applications of NumPy. Its versatility, efficiency, and powerful array operations make it an essential library in many fields that require numerical computation and data analysis.

# CHAPTER IX

# I/O and Regular Expressions

## 9.1 Data File Handling

Data stored in variables and lists is temporary — it's lost when the program terminates. Python allows a program to read data from a file or write data to a file. Once the data is saved in a file on computer disk, it will remain there after the program stops running. The data can then be retrieved and used at a later time. There are two types of files in Python - text files and binary files.

A text file is processed as a sequence of characters. In a text file there is a special end-of-line symbol that divides file into lines. In addition, you can think that there is a special end-of-file symbol that follows the last component in a file. A big advantage of text files is that it may be opened and viewed in a text editor such as Notepad.

## 9.2 Text files in Python

Text files don't have any specific encoding and it can be opened in normal text editor itself.

Example:

- Web standards: html, XML, CSS, JSON etc.
- Source code: c, app, js, py, java etc.
- Documents: txt, tex, RTF etc.
- Tabular data: csv, tsv etc.
- Configuration: ini, cfg, reg etc.

A binary file stores data that has not been translated into character form. Binary files typically use the same bit patterns to represent data as those used to represent the data in the computer's main memory. These files are called binary files because the only thing they have in common is that they store the data as sequences of zeros and ones.

## 9.3 Binary files in Python

Most of the files that we see in our computer system are called binary files.

Example:

- Document files: .pdf, .doc, .xls etc.
- Image files: .png, .jpg, .gif, .bmp etc.
- Video files: .mp4, .3gp, .mkv, .avi etc.
- Audio files: .mp3, .wav, .mka, .aac etc.
- Database files: .mdb, .accde, .frm, .sqlite etc.
- Archive files: .zip, .rar, .iso, .7z etc.
- Executable files: .exe, .dll, .class etc.

### Steps to process file Input/output in Python

Step 1. Open the file — Opening a file creates a connection between the file and the program.

Step 2. Process the file — In this step data is either written to the file (if it is an output file) or read from the file (if it is an input file).

Step 3. Close the file — When the program is finished using the file, the file must be closed. Closing a file disconnects the file from the program.

### Open() Function

Python has an in-built function called open() to open a file. It takes a minimum of one argument as mentioned in the below syntax. The open method returns a file object which is used to access the write, read and other in-built methods.Here is the general format:

```
File_object=open(file_name,mode)
```

**file mode**

- 'r' – Read Mode: Read mode is used only to read data from the file.
- 'w' – Write Mode: This mode is used when you want to write data into the file or modify it. Remember write mode overwrites the data present in the file.
- 'a' – Append Mode: Append mode is used to append data to the file. Remember data will be appended at the end of the file pointer.
- 'r+' – Read or Write Mode: This mode is used when we want to write or read the data from the same file.
- 'a+' – Append or Read Mode: This mode is used when we want to read data from the file or append the data into the same file.

In addition you can specify if the file should be handled as binary or text mode.

- 't' - Text mode
- 'b' - Binary mode

The text mode is the default. So, you do not need to specify that.

While using binary files, we have to use the same modes with the letter 'b' at the end. So that Python can understand that we are interacting with binary files.

- 'wb' – Open a file for write only mode in the binary format.
- 'rb' – Open a file for the read-only mode in the binary format.
- 'ab' – Open a file for appending only mode in the binary format.
- 'rb+' – Open a file for read and write only mode in the binary format.
- 'ab+' – Open a file for appending and read-only mode in the binary format.

## 9.4 Python Read from File

In order to read a file in python, we must open the file in read mode.

There are three ways in which we can read the files in python.

- read([n])
- readline([n])
- readlines()

Here, n is the number of bytes to be read.

First, let's create a sample text file as shown below.



Now let's observe what each read method does:

Example 1:

```
my_file = open("D:\kk.txt", "r")
print(my_file.read())
```

Output:

```
Hello World
Hello Python
Good Morning
```

Here we have not provided any argument inside the read() function. Hence it will read all the content present inside the file.

Example 2:

```
my_file = open("D:\kk.txt", "r")
print(my_file.read(5))
```

Output:

```
Hello
```

Here we are opening the file test.txt in a read-only mode and are reading only the first 5 characters of the file using the my_file.read(5) method.

Example 4:

```
my_file  = open("D:\kk.txt",  "r")
print(my_file.readline())
                                        Output:
                            Hello  World
```

Using this function we can read the content of the file on a line by line basis.

Example 3:

```
my_file  = open("D:\kk.txt",  "r")
print(my_file.readline(2))
                                        Output:
                                    He
```

This function returns the first 2 characters of the next line.

Example 5:

```
my_file = open("D:\kk.txt", "r")
print(my_file.readlines())
                                        Output:
    ['Hello World\n', 'Hello Python\n', 'Good Morning']
```

Here we are reading all the lines present inside the text file including the newline characters.

**9.5 Writing Data to a Text File**

The following program writes the name of four persons to the text file. We have two methods for writing data into a file as shown below.

- write(string)
- writelines(list)

Program (names.py)

```
outfile = open('names.txt', 'w')   #Step 1
outfile.write('Kartheeban\n')    #Step 2
outfile.write('K. P. Dharsini\n')
outfile.write('K. P. Kowshik\n')
outfile.write('Meena\n')
outfile.close()          #Step 3
```

Output

On running this program a new text file 'names.txt' is created and stored in same folder where you have saved 'names.py'. Now discuss the above prgram step by step:

Step 1

*outfile = open('names.txt', 'w')*          *#Step 1*

open function creates the file 'oceans.txt' and returns the file object to outfile. 'w' is file mode used for writing to text file.

Step 2

*outfile.write('Atlantic\n')*          *#Step 2*

The above statement writes the contents of string to the file.

Step 3                              *outfile.close()*

outfile.close() is used to close the file and immediately free up any system resources used by it.

## 9.6 Relative and Absolute Path

Relative Path: A relative path is the path that is relative to the working directory location on your computer. In Program (oceans.py) we have used relative path of ocean.txt in open function. Therfore, text file 'oceans.txt' is created and stored in same folder (current working directory) where we have saved 'oceans.py'

Absolute Path: An absolute path is a path that contains the entire path to the file that you need to access. This path will begin with drive of your computer and will end with the file that you wish to access. Example:

*D:\names.txt*

```
outfile = open('D:\names.txt', 'w')            #Step 1
outfile.write('Kartheeban\n')                  #Step 2
outfile.write('K.P.Dharsini\n')
outfile.write('K.P.Kowshik\n')
outfile.write('Meena\n')

outfile.close()                                #Step 3
```

Example 1:

```
my_file = open("D:/test.txt", "w")
my_file.write("Hello World")
```

The above code writes the String 'Hello World' into the 'test.txt' file.

**Before writing data to a test.txt file:**

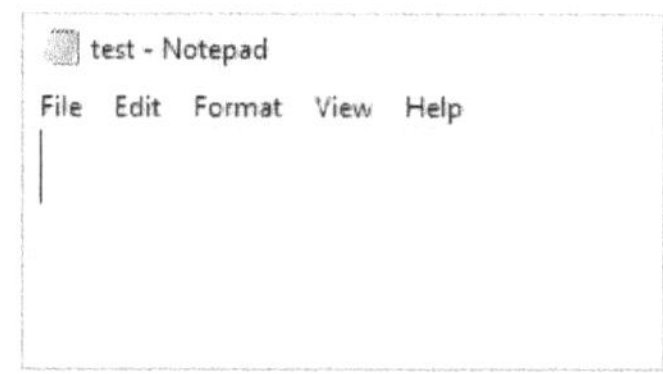


Output:



Example 2:

```
my_file = open("D:/test.txt", "w")
my_file.write("Hello World\n")
my_file.write("Hello Python")
```

The first line will be 'Hello World' and as we have mentioned \n character, the cursor will move to the next line of the file and then write 'Hello Python'. Remember if we don't mention \n character, then the data will be written continuously in the text file like 'Hello WorldHelloPython'

Output:

Example 3:

```
fruits = ["Apple\n", "Orange\n", "Grapes\n", "Watermelon"]
my_file = open("D:/test.txt", "w")
my_file.writelines(fruits)
```

The above code writes a list of data into the 'test.txt' file simultaneously.

Output:

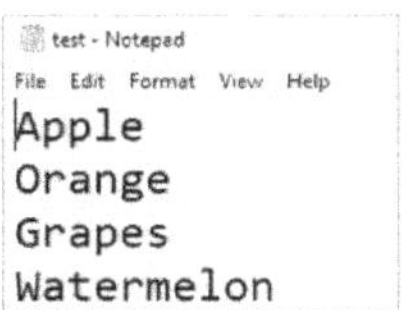



## 9.7 Python Append to File

To append data into a file we must open the file in 'a+' mode so that we will have access to both the append as well as write modes.

Example 1:

```
my_file = open("D:/test.txt", "a+")
my_file.write("Strawberry")
```

The above code appends the string 'Apple' at the end of the 'test.txt' file.

Output:

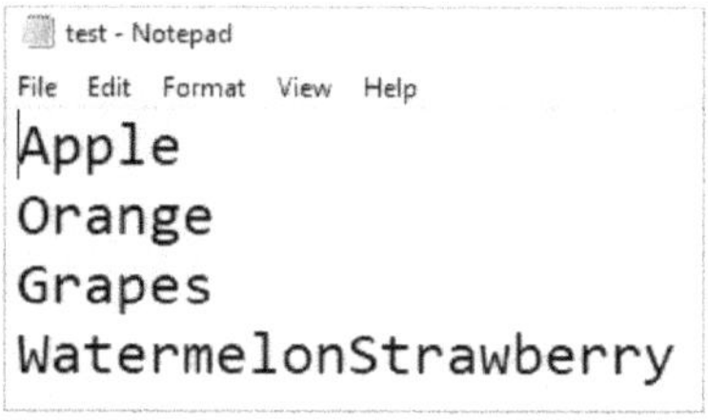

```
test - Notepad
File  Edit  Format  View  Help
Apple
Orange
Grapes
WatermelonStrawberry
```

Example 2:

```
my_file = open("D:/test.txt", "a+")
my_file.write ("\nGuava")
```

The above code appends the string 'Apple' at the end of the 'test.txt' file in a new line.

Output:

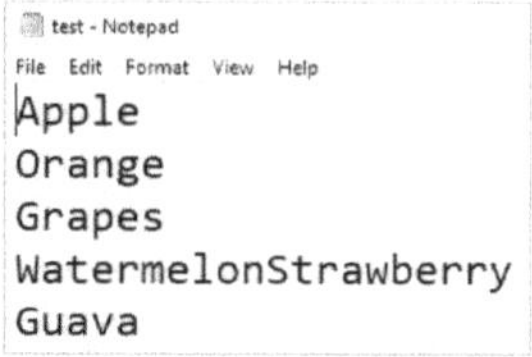

```
test - Notepad
File  Edit  Format  View  Help
Apple
Orange
Grapes
WatermelonStrawberry
Guava
```

Example 3:

```
fruits = ["\nBanana", "\nAvocado", "\nFigs", "\nMango"]
my_file = open("D:/test.txt", "a+")
my_file.writelines(fruits)
```

The above code appends a list of data into a 'test.txt' file.

```
test - Notepad
File  Edit  Format  View  Help
Apple
Orange
Grapes
WatermelonStrawberry
Guava
Banana
Avocado
Figs
Mango
```

Example 4:

```python
text=["\nHello","\nHi","\nPython"]
my_file=open("C:/Documents/Python/test.txt",mode="a+")
my_file.writelines(text)
print("where the file cursor is: ",my_file.tell())
my_file.seek(0)
for line in my_file:
    print(line)
```

In the above code, we are appending the list of data into the 'test.txt' file. Here, you can observe that we have used the tell() method which prints where the cursor is currently at.

seek(offset): The offset takes three types of arguments namely 0,1 and 2.

When the offset is 0: Reference will be pointed at the beginning of the file.

When the offset is 1: Reference will be pointed at the current cursor position.

When the offset is 2: Reference will be pointed at the end of the file.

```python
text = ["\nHello", "\nHi", "\nPython"]
my_file = open("C:/Documents/Python/test.txt", mode="a+")
my_file.writelines(text)
print("where the file cursor is:", my_file.tell())
my_file.seek(0)
for line in my_file:
    print(line)
```

Output:

```
where the file cursor is: 99
Apple

Orange

Grapes

WatermelonStrawberry

Guava

Banana

Avocado

Figs

Mango

Hello

Hi

Python

Process finished with exit code 0
```

## 9.8 Python Close File

In order to close a file, we must first open the file. In python, we have an in-built method called close() to close the file which is opened. Whenever you open a file, it is important to close it, especially, with write method. Because if we don't call the close function after the write method then whatever data we have written to a file will not be saved into the file.

Example 1:

```python
my_file = open("C:/Documents/Python/test.txt", "r")
print(my_file.read())
my_file.close()
```

Example 2:

```
my_file = open("C:/Documents/Python/test.txt", "w")
my_file.write("Hello World")
my_file.close()
```

## 9.9 Python Rename or Delete File

Python provides us with an "os" module which has some in-built methods that would help us in performing the file operations such as renaming and deleting the file. In order to use this module, first of all, we need to import the "os" module in our program and then call the related methods.

rename() method:

This rename() method accepts two arguments i.e. the current file name and the new file name.

Syntax:

```
os.rename(current_file_name, new_file_name)
```

Example 1:

```
import os
os.rename("D:\test.txt", "D:\test1.txt")
```

Here 'test.txt' is the current file name and 'test1.txt' is the new file name. You can specify the location as well as shown in the below example.

Example 2:

```
import os
os.rename("D:/test.txt", "D:/test1.txt")
```

**remove() method:**

We use the remove() method to delete the file by supplying the file name or the file location that you want to delete.

Syntax:

```
os.remove(file_name)
```

Example 1:

```
import os
os.remove("D:\test.txt")
```

Here 'test.txt' is the file that you want to remove. Similarly, we can pass the file location as well to the arguments as shown in the below example

Example 2:

```
import os
os.remove("D:/test.txt")
```

## 9.10 Writing and Reading Data from a Binary File

Binary files store data in the binary format (0's and 1's) which is understandable by the machine. So when we open the binary file in our machine, it decodes the data and displays in a human-readable format.

Example:

#Let's create some binary file.

```
my_file = open("D:/bfile.bin", "wb+")
message = "Hello Python"
file_encode = message.encode("ASCII")
my_file.write(file_encode)
my_file.seek(0)
bdata = my_file.read()
print("Binary Data:", bdata)
ntext = bdata.decode("ASCII")
print("Normal data:", ntext)
```

In the above example, first we are creating a binary file 'bfile.bin' with the read and write access and whatever data you want to enter into the file must be encoded before you call the write method.

Also, we are printing the data without decoding it, so that we can observe how the data exactly looks inside the file when it's encoded and we are also printing the same data by decoding it so that it can be readable by humans.

Output:

Binary Data: b'Hello Python'

Normal data: Hello Python

## 9.11 File I/O Attributes

| Attribute | Description |
| --- | --- |
| Name | Return the name of the file |
| Mode | Return mode of the file |
| Encoding | Return the encoding format of the file |
| Closed | Return true if the file closed else returns false |

Example:

```
my_file = open("D:/test.txt", "a+")
print("What is the file name? ", my_file.name)
print("What is the file mode? ", my_file.mode)
print("What is the encoding format? ", my_file.encoding)
print("Is File closed? ", my_file.closed)
my_file.close()
print("Is File closed? ", my_file.closed)
```

Output:

What is the file name? D:/test.txt
What is the file mode? r
What is the encoding format? cp1252
Is File closed? False
Is File closed? True
Let's try out a few other methods of the file.

Example:

```
my_file = open("D:/test.txt", "w+")
my_file.write("Hello Python\nHello World\nGood Morning")
my_file.seek(0)
print(my_file.read())
print("Is file readable: ?", my_file.readable())
print("Is file writeable: ?", my_file.writable())
print("File no:", my_file.fileno())
my_file.close()
```

Output:

*Hello Python*
*Hello World*
*Good Morning*
*Is file readable:? True*
*Is file writeable:? True*
*File no: 3*

## 9.12 Python File Methods

| Function | Explanation |
|---|---|
| open() | To open a file |
| close() | Close an open file |
| fileno() | Returns an integer number of the file |
| read(n) | Reads 'n' characters from the file till end of the file |
| readable() | Returns true if the file is readable |
| readline() | Read and return one line from the file |
| readlines() | Reads and returns all the lines from the file |
| seek(offset) | Change the cursor position by bytes as specified by the offset |
| seekable() | Returns true if the file supports random access |
| tell() | Returns the current file location |
| writable() | Returns true if the file is writable |
| write() | Writes a string of data to the file |
| writelines() | Writes a list of data to the file |

Let's see what we have discussed so far in an end-end program.

Example:

```python
my_file = open("D:/test.txt", mode="w+")
print("What is the file name? ", my_file.name)
print("What is the mode of the file? ", my_file.mode)
print("What is the encoding format?", my_file.encoding)

text = ["Hello Python\n", "Good Morning\n", "Good Bye"]
my_file.writelines(text)

print("Size of the file is: ", my_file.__sizeof__())
print("Cursor position is at byte: ", my_file.tell())
my_file.seek(0)
print("Content of the file is: ", my_file.read())
my_file.close()

file = open("D:/test.txt", mode="r")
line_number = 3
current_line = 1
data = 0
for line in file:
    if current_line == line_number:
        data = line
        print("Data present at current line is: ", data)
        break
    current_line = current_line + 1

bin_file = open("D:/bfile.exe", mode="wb+")
message_content = data.encode("utf-32")
bin_file.write(message_content)
bin_file.seek(0)
bdata = bin_file.read()
print("Binary Data is: ", bdata)
ndata = bdata.decode("utf-32")
print("Normal Data is: ", ndata)
file.close()
bin_file.close()
```

Output:

*What is the file name? C:/Documents/Python/test.txt*
*What is the mode of the file? w+*
*What is the encoding format? cp1252*
*Size of the file is: 192*
*Cursor position is at byte: 36*

*Content of the file is: Hello Python*
*Good Morning*
*Good Bye*
*Data present at the current line is: Good Bye*
*Binary                              Data                              is:*
*b'\xff\xfe\x00\x00G\x00\x00\x00o\x00\x00\x00o\x00\x00\x00d\x0*
*0\x00\x00*
*\x00\x00\x00B\x00\x00\x00y\x00\x00\x00e\x00\x00\x00'*
*Normal Data is: Good Bye*

**rstrip()**

Output of above program shows extra spances between lines. This is because readline() method reads the string including the \n. However, in many cases you want to remove the \n from a string after it is read from a file. In Python rstrip() method removes specific characters from the end of a string.

```
infile = open('D:\karthee.txt', 'r')
line1 = infile.readline().rstrip('\n')
line2 = infile.readline().rstrip('\n')
line3 = infile.readline().rstrip('\n')
print(line1)
print(line2)
print(line3)
infile.close()
```

for Loop to Read All Lines from the file

```
file = open('D:\karthee.txt', 'r')

for line in file:
    line = line.rstrip()
    print(line)

file.close()
```

Output

*Atlantic*
*Pacific*

*Indian*
*Arctic*
*Southern*

The first time the loop iterates, the line variable will reference the first line in the file, the second time the loop iterates, the line variable will reference the second line, and so forth. Remember that the line variable will contain the trailing new line character, e.g. "Atlantic\n"

1.Write a method in python to write multiple line of text contents into a text file mylife.txt.

```python
def writelines():
    outfile = open('D:\myfile.txt', 'w')

    while True:
        line = input('Enter line: ')
        line += '\n'
        outfile.write(line)
        choice = input('Are there more lines y/n? ')
        if choice == 'n':
            break
    outfile.close()

# Call the writelines function.
writelines()
```

Output

*Enter line: Beautiful is better than ugly.*
*Are there more lines y/n? y*
*Enter line: Explicit is better than implicit.*
*Are there more lines y/n? y*
*Enter line: Simple is better than complex.*
*Are there more lines y/n? n*

2. Write a function in Phyton to read lines from a text file diary.txt, and display only those lines, which are starting with an alphabet 'P'.

If the contents of file is :

I hope you will please write to me from all the cities you visit. Please accept them with the love and good wishes of your friend. He never thought something so simple could please him so much.

```python
def readlines():
    file = open('D:\diary.txt', 'r')
    for line in file:
        if line[0] == 'P':
            print(line)

    file.close()

# Call the readlines function
readlines()
```

3. Assuming that a text file named first.txt contains some text written into it, write a function that reads the file first.txt and creates a new file named second.txt, to contain only those words from the file first.txt which start with a lowercase vowel (i.e. with 'a', 'e', 'i', 'o', 'u').

For example if the file first.txt contains

Carry umbrella and overcoat when it rains
Then the file second.txt shall contain
umbrella and overcoat it

```python
def copy_file():
    infile = open('D:\first.txt', 'r')
    outfile = open('second.txt', 'w')

    for line in infile:
        words = line.split()
        for word in words:
            if word[0] in 'aeiou':
                outfile.write(word + ' ')

    infile.close()
    outfile.close()

# Call the copy_file function
copy_file()
```

4. Write a function in Python to count and display number of vowels in text file.

```python
def count_vowels():
    infile = open('D:\first.txt', 'r')
    count = 0
    data = infile.read()
    for letter in data:
        if letter in 'aeiouAEIOU':
            count += 1

    print('Number of vowels are', count)
    infile.close()

# Call the count_vowels function
count_vowels()
```

# CHAPTER X

## Pickling

Pickling is the act of converting objects to a stream of bytes. You can use in-built module pickle to flatten complex object hierarchies into a byte stream. Unpickling is the inverse operation, whereby a byte stream is converted back into an object hierarchy. Pickling is alternatively known as "serialization", "marshalling", or "flattening".

To serialize (pickle) an object hierarchy, you simply call the dump() function. Similarly, to de-serialize a data stream, you call the load() function.

You can pickle any object like integers, strings, tuples, lists, dictionaries, etc. and save it in a binary file.

### 10.1 Pickling a dictionary object and writing to file

The following program demonstrates how to pickle(serialize) dictionary object and write the object into the binary file.

```
import pickle

#create a dictionary
phonebook = {
    'Kartheeban': 759818 2878,
    'Dharsini': 9487339992,
    'John': 87989898
}
#open file in binary mode for writing.
outfile = open('D:\phonebook.dat', 'wb')

#serialize the object and writing to file
pickle.dump(phonebook, outfile)

#close the file
outfile.close()
```

## 10. 2 Reading from File and unpickling the dictionary object

The following program demonstrates how to read data from binary file and unpickle it.

```python
import pickle

#open file in binary mode for reading
infile = open('D:\phonebook.dat', 'rb')
#reading the oject from file
phonebook = pickle.load(infile)
#display the phonebook
print(phonebook)

#close the file
infile.close()
```

## Pickling and unpickling the list object using file

```python
import pickle

def write_record():
    #opening a binary file in write mode
    outfile = open('student.dat','wb')
    #creating a list object
    student = [1,'Nisha','XII']
    #writing to file
    pickle.dump(student,outfile)
    #close the file
    outfile.close()

def read_record():
    #opening the binary file in read mode
    infile = open('student.dat','rb')
    #read object from file and unpickle
    student = pickle.load(infile)
    #display student record
    print(student)
    #close the file
    infile.close()


write_record()

read_record()
```

5.Write a menu driven program in Python that asks the user to add, display, and search records of employee stored in a binary file. The employee record contains employee code, name and salary. It should be stored in a list object. Your program should pickle the object and save it to a binary file.

```python
def display_data(employee):
    print('Employee code:', employee[0])
    print('Employee name:', employee[1])
    print('Salary:', employee[2])
    print()
def write_record():
    #open file in binary mode for writing
    outfile = open('emp.dat', 'ab')
    #serialize the object and writing to file
    pickle.dump(set_data(), outfile)

    #close the file
    outfile.close()
def read_records():
    #open file in binary mode for reading
    infile = open('emp.dat', 'rb')

    #read to the end of file.
    while True:
        try:
            #reading the oject from file
            employee = pickle.load(infile)

            #display the object
            display_data(employee)
        except EOFError:
            break
    #close the file
    infile.close()
def search_record():
    infile = open('emp.dat', 'rb')
    empcode = int(input('Enter employee code to search: '))
    flag = False

    #read to the end of file.
    while True:
        try:
            #reading the oject from file
            employee = pickle.load(infile)

            #display record if found and set flag
            if employee[0] == empcode:
                display_data(employee)
                flag = True
                break
        except EOFError:
            break


    if flag == False:
```

```python
    if flag == False:
        print('Record not Found')
        print()

    #close the file
    infile.close()

def show_choices():
    print('Menu')
    print('1. Add Record')
    print('2. Display Records')
    print('3. Search a Record')
    print('4. Exit')

def main():
    while(True):
        show_choices()
        choice = input('Enter choice(1-4): ')
        print()

        if choice == '1':
            write_record()

        elif choice == '2':
            read_records()

        elif choice == '3':
            search_record()

        elif choice == '4':
            break

        else:
            print('Invalid input')

#call the main function.
main()
```

## 10.3 Solved Programs

1. Write a function in python to read the content from a text file "karthee.txt" line by line and display the same on screen.

Source Code:

```
def readAndDisplay_file():
    file = open("D:\karthee.txt","r")
    line=file.read()
    for line in file:
        print(line, end="")
    file.close()
readAndDisplay_file()
```

2. Write a function in python to count the number of lines from a text file "karthee1.txt" which is not starting with an alphabet "T". Example: If the file "karthee1.txt" contains the following lines:

My son name is K.P.Kowshik.
There is a playground.
And he is studying 9th STD at Y.R.T.V.MATRIC.
The sky is UNLIMITED.

Alphabets and numbers are allowed in the password.

Source Code:

```
def count_line():
    fp = open("D:\karthee1.txt","r")
    count=0
    for line in fp:
        if line[0] not in 'T':
            count+= 1
    fp.close()

    print("No of lines not starting with 'T'=",count)

count_line()
```

3. Write a function in Python to count and display the total number of words in a text file.

Source Code:

```python
def words_count():
    fp = open("D:\karthee1.txt","r")
    count = 0
    for line in fp:
        words = line.split()
        for i in words:
            count += 1
    print("Total words are",count)
words_count()
```

4. Write a function in Python to read lines from a text file "karthee2.txt". Your function should find and display the occurrence of the word "the". For example: If the content of the file is:

"India is the fastest-growing economy. India is looking for more investments around the globe. The whole world is looking at India as a great market. Most of the Indians can foresee the heights that India is capable of reaching."

Source Code:

```python
def words_count():
    fp = open("D:\karthee2.txt","r")
    count = 0
    for line in fp:
        words = line.split()
        for word in words:
            if word =="the" or word =="The":
                count += 1
    print("Total words are",count)
words_count()
```

5. Write a function display_words() in python to read lines from a text file "karthee.txt", and display those words, which are less than 4 characters.

Source Code:

```
def Display_words():
    file = open("D:\karthee.txt","r")
    for line in file:
        words=line.split()
        for word in words:
            if len(line)<4:
            print(line, end="")
    file.close()

Display_words()
```

6. Write a function in Python to count the words "this" and "these" present in a text file "karthee4.txt". [Note that the words "this" and "these" are complete words]

Source Code:

```
def words_count():
    fp = open("D:\karthee2.txt","r")
    count = 0
    for line in fp:
        words = line.split()
        for i in words:
            if i=='this' or i=='these'
            count += 1
    print("Total words are",count)
words_count()
```

7. Write a function in Python to count words in a text file those are ending with alphabet "r".

Source Code:

```
def count_words():
    file = open("D:\karthee2.txt","r")
    count = 0
    for line in file:
        words = line.split()
        for word in words:
            if word[-1] == 'r':
                count+=1

    print(count)
```

8. Write a function in Python to count uppercase character in a text file.

Source Code:

```
def count_letter():
    file = open("D:karthee2.txt","r")
    data = file.read()
    count = 0
    for letter in data:
        if letter.isupper():
            count+=1
    print(count)
count_letter()
```

9. A text file named "kk.txt" contains some text, which needs to be displayed such that every next character is separated by a symbol "*". Write a function definition for astrix_display () in Python that would display the entire content of the file kk.txt in the desired format.  Example:  If the file kk.txt has the following content stored in it:

PYTHON PROGRAMMING.  The function astrix_display () should display the following content : P*Y*T*H*O*N*P*R*O*G*R*A*M*M*I*N*G

Source Code:

```
def astrix_display():
    file = open("D:\kk.txt", "r")
    data = file.read()
    for letter in data:
        print(letter, end="*")
    file.close()
astrix_display()
```

10. Kartheeban has used a text editing software to type some text. After saving the article as  project.txt, he realized that he has wrongly typed alphabet J in place of alphabet I everywhere in the article. Write a function definition for convert_J_TO_I() in Python that would display the corrected version of entire content of the file project.txt with all the alphabets "J" to be displayed as an alphabet "I" on screen. Note: Assuming that project.txt does not contain any J alphabet otherwise.

Example: If kartheeban has stored the following content in the file project.txt:

WELL, THJS JS A WORD BY JTSELF. YOU COULD STRETCH THJS TO BE A SENTENCE.

The function convert_J_TO_I() should display the following content:

WELL, THIS IS A WORD BY ITSELF. YOU COULD STRETCH THIS TO BE A SENTENCE

Source Code:

```
def convert_J_TO_I():
    file = open("d:\project.txt","r")
    data = file.read()
    for letter in data:
        if letter == 'J':
            print("I",end="")
        else:
            print(letter,end="")
    file.close()
convert_J_TO_I()
```

11. Write a function Count_AaMm() in Python, which should read each character of a text file kk3.txt, should count and display the occurance of alphabets A and M (including small cases a and m too). For example:If the file content is as follows:

Updated information

As simplified by official websites. The Count_AaMm() function should display the output as:

A or a:4
M or m :2
Source Code:

```python
def Count_AaMm():
    file = open('D:\kk3.txt', 'r')
    data = file.read()
    counta=0
    countm=0
    for letter in data:
        if letter == 'A' or letter =='a':
            counta += 1
        elif letter == 'M' or letter =='m':
            countm += 1

    file.close()
    print('A or a:',counta)
    print('M or m:',countm)

Count_AaMm()
```

12. A binary file "Book.dat" has structure [BookNo, Book_Name, Author, Price].

- o Write a user defined function createFile() to input data for a record and add to Book.dat.
- o Write a function countRec(Author) in Python which accepts the Author name as parameter and count and return number of books by the given Author are stored in the binary file "Book.dat"

Source Code:

```python
import pickle
def createFile():
    file = open("book.dat", "ab")
    BookNo = int(input("Enter book number: "))
    Book_Name = input("Enter book Name: ")
    Author =input("Enter author: ")
    Price = int(input("Enter price: "))
    record = [BookNo, Book_Name, Author, Price]
    pickle.dump(record, file)
    file.close()
def countRec(Author):
    file = open("book.dat", "rb")
    count = 0
    try:
        while True:
            record = pickle.load(file)
            if record[2]==Author:
                count+=1
    except EOFError:
        pass
    return count
    file.close()

#To test working of functions
def testProgram():
    while True:
        createFile()
        choice = input("Add more record (y/n)? ")
        if choice in 'Nn':
            break
    Author = input('Enter author name to search: ')
    n = countRec(Author)
    print("No of books are ",n)

testProgram()
```

```
def count_rec():
  file = open("STUDENT.DAT", "rb")
  count = 0
  try:
    while True:
      record = pickle.load(file)
      if record[2] > 75:
        print(record)
        count+=1
  except EOFError:
    pass
  print('No of students having more than 75% are', count)
  file.close()
```

13. A binary file "STUDENT.DAT" has structure (admission_number, Name, Percentage). Write a function count_rec() in Python that would read contents of the file "STUDENT.DAT" and display the details of those students whose percentage is above 75. Also display number of students scoring above 75%.

```
def count_rec():
  file = open("STUDENT.DAT","rb")
  count = 0
  try:
    while True:
      record = pickle.load(file)
      if record[2] > 75:
        print(record)
        count+=1
  except EOFError:
    pass
  print('No of students having more than 75% are', count)
```

14. Given a binary file employee.dat, created using dictionary object having keys: (empcode, name, and salary). (i)Write a python function that adds one more record at the end of file.

(ii)Write a python function that display all employee records whose salary is more than 30000

```python
import pickle
def add_record():
    file = open("employee.dat","ab")
    emp = {}
    emp['empcode'] = int(input("Enter employee code: "))
    emp['name'] = input("Enter employee Name: ")
    emp['salary'] = int(input("Enter salary: "))
    pickle.dump(emp, file)
    file.close()
def search():
    file = open("employee.dat","rb")
    try:
        while True:
            emp = pickle.load(file)
            if emp['salary']>30000:
                print(emp)
    except EOFError:
        pass
    file.close()
#To test working of functions
def testProgram():
    while True:
        add_record()
        choice = input("Add more record (y/n)? ")
        if choice in 'Nn':
            break
    print('Employee details having salary more than 30000')
    search()
testProgram()
```

15. Write a function to search and display details of student whose rollno is '1005' from the binary file student.dat having structure [rollno, name, class and fees].

Source Code:

```python
def search():
    file = open("student.dat","rb")
    try:
        while True:
            record = pickle.load(file)
            if record[0] == 1005:
                print(record)
    except EOFError:
        pass
    file.close()
```

16. A binary file school.dat has structure (rollno, name, class, fees)

Write a definition for function total_fees( ) that reads each object of file and calculate the total fees of students and display the same.

Source Code:

```
def total_fees():
    file = open("school.dat","rb")
    try:
        total = 0
        while True:
            record = pickle.load(file)
            total += record[3]:
    except EOFError:
        pass
    print('Total Fees: ',total)
    file.close()
```

17. Given a binary file game.dat, containing records of following list format: [game_name, participants]. Write a function in Python that would read contents from the file game.dat and creates a file named basket.dat copying only those records from game.dat where the game name is "Basket Ball"

Source Code:

```
def countRec(country):
    infile = open("game.dat","rb")
    outfile = open("basket.dat","wb")
    try:
        while True:
            record = pickle.load(infile)
            if record[0] == "Basket Ball":
                pickle.dump(record, outfile)
    except EOFError:
        pass
    infile.close()
    outfile.close()
```

18. A binary file players.dat, containing records of following list format: [code, name, country and total runs] (i)Write a python function that display all records where player name starts from 'A' (ii)Write a python function that accept country as an argument and count and display the number of players of that country. (iii)Write a python function that add one record at the end of file.

Source Code:

```python
import pickle
def createFile():
file = open("players.dat", "ab")
Code = int(input("Enter player code: "))
Name = input("Enter player Name: ")
Country = input("Enter player country: ")
Total_Runs = int(input("Enter total runs of player: "))
record = [Code, Name, Country, Total_Runs]
pickle.dump(record, file)
file.close()
def search():
file = open("players.dat", "rb")
try:
while True:
record = pickle.load(file)
if record[1][0] == 'A':
print(record)
except EOFError:
pass
file.close()
def countRec(Country):
file = open("players.dat", "rb")
count = 0
try:
while True:
record = pickle.load(file)
if record[2]==Country:
count+=1
except EOFError:
pass
return count
file.close()

def testProgram():
while True:
createFile()
choice = input("Add more record (y/n)? ")
if choice in 'Nn':
break
print("the number of players whose name starts with
A: ", search())
Country = input('Enter country name to search: ')

n = countRec(Country)

print("No of players are ", n)

testProgram()
```

# CHAPTER XI

# Data Structures and GUI, CGI Scripts

## 11.1 Comprehensions in Python

Comprehensions in Python provide us with a short and concise way to construct new sequences (such as lists, set, dictionary etc.) using sequences which have been already defined. Python supports the following 4 types of comprehensions:

- List Comprehensions
- Dictionary Comprehensions
- Set Comprehensions
- Generator Comprehensions

## 11.2 List Comprehensions

List comprehensions allow you to create a new list by applying an expression to each element of an existing iterable (e.g., list, tuple, or string). The basic syntax for a list comprehension is enclosed in square brackets [] and consists of an expression followed by a for loop that iterates over the elements of the existing iterable. Note that list comprehension may or may not contain an if condition. List comprehensions can contain multiple for (nested list comprehensions).

```
output_list = [output_exp for var in input_list if (var satisfies this condition)]
```

Example #1: Suppose we want to create an output list which contains only the even numbers which are present in the input list. Let's see how to do this using for loops and list comprehension and decide which method suits better.

#constructing output list WITHOUT Using List comprehensions

```
input_list = [1, 2, 3, 4, 4, 5, 6, 7, 7]
output_list = []

# Using loop for constructing output list
for var in input_list:
        if var % 2 == 0:
                output_list.append(var)
print("Output List using for loop: ", output_list)

                                                  Output:
                                Output List using for loop: [2, 4, 4, 6]
```

# Using List comprehensions for constructing output list

```
input_list = [1, 2, 3, 4, 4, 5, 6, 7, 7]
list_using_comp = [var for var in input_list if var % 2 == 0]
print("Output List using list comprehensions: ", list_using_comp)
                                                  Output:
                        Output List using list comprehensions: [2, 4, 4, 6]
```

Example #2: Suppose we want to create an output list which contains squares of all the numbers from 1 to 9. Let's see how to do this using for loops and list comprehension.

```
# Constructing output list using for loop
output_list = []
for var in range(1, 10):
        output_list.append(var ** 2)
print("Output List using for loop: ", output_list)


                                                  Output:
                Output List using for loop: [1, 4, 9, 16, 25, 36, 49, 64, 81]
```

```
# Constructing output list using list comprehension
list_using_comp = [var**2 for var in range(1, 10)]
print("Output List using list comprehension: ", list_using_comp)

                                                  Output:
                Output List using list comprehension: [1, 4, 9, 16, 25, 36, 49, 64, 81]
```

```
# Constructing output list using list comprehension
numbers = [1, 2, 3, 4, 5]
squared_numbers = [num**2 for num in numbers]
print(squared_numbers)
                                                    Output:
                                              [1, 4, 9, 16, 25]
```

## 11.3 Nested List Comprehensions in Python

List comprehensions are one of the most amazing features of Python. It is a smart and concise way of creating lists by iterating over an iterable object. Nested List Comprehensions are nothing but a list comprehension within another list comprehension which is quite similar to nested for loops. Let's take a look at some examples to understand what nested list comprehensions can do:

Example 1:

I want to create a matrix which looks like below:

matrix = [[0, 1, 2, 3, 4],

      [0, 1, 2, 3, 4],

      [0, 1, 2, 3, 4],

      [0, 1, 2, 3, 4],

      [0, 1, 2, 3, 4]]

The below code uses nested for loops for the given task:

```
matrix = []
for i in range(5):
        # Append an empty sublist inside the list
        matrix.append([])
        for j in range(5):
                matrix[i].append(j)
print(matrix)
                                                    Output:
    [[0, 1, 2, 3, 4], [0, 1, 2, 3, 4], [0, 1, 2, 3, 4], [0, 1, 2, 3, 4],
                                              [0, 1, 2, 3, 4]]
```

## 11.4 Dictionary Comprehensions:

Extending the idea of list comprehensions, we can also create a dictionary using dictionary comprehensions. The basic structure of a dictionary comprehension looks like below.

```
output_dict = {key:value for (key, value) in iterable if (key, va
lue satisfy this condition)}
```

Example #1: Suppose we want to create an output dictionary which contains only the odd numbers that are present in the input list as keys and their cubes as values. Let's see how to do this using for loops and dictionary comprehension.

```
input_list = [1, 2, 3, 4, 5, 6, 7]
output_dict = {}
# Using loop for constructing output dictionary
for var in input_list:
        if var % 2 != 0:
                output_dict[var] = var**3
print("Output Dictionary using for loop:",output_dict )

                                                Output:
        Output Dictionary using for loop: {1: 1, 3: 27, 5: 125, 7: 343}
```

# using Dictionary comprehensions for constructing output dictionary

```
input_list = [1,2,3,4,5,6,7]
dict_using_comp = {var:var ** 3 for var in input_list if var % 2 != 0}
print("Output Dictionary using dictionary comprehensions:",dict_using_comp)

                                                Output:
    Output Dictionary using dictionary comprehensions: {1: 1, 3: 27, 5: 125, 7:
                                                        343}
```

Example #2: Given two lists containing the names of states and their corresponding capitals, construct a dictionary which maps the states with their respective capitals. Let's see how to do this using for loops and dictionary comprehension.

```
state = ['Gujarat', 'Maharashtra', 'Rajasthan']
capital = ['Gandhinagar', 'Mumbai', 'Jaipur']
output_dict = {}
# Using loop for constructing output dictionary
for (key, value) in zip(state, capital):
        output_dict[key] = value
print("Output Dictionary using for loop:", output_dict)

                                                Output:
    Output Dictionary using for loop: {'Gujarat': 'Gandhinagar',
                        'Maharashtra': 'Mumbai', 'Rajasthan': 'Jaipur'}
```

# Using Dictionary comprehensions for constructing output dictionary

```
state = ['Gujarat', 'Maharashtra', 'Rajasthan']
capital = ['Gandhinagar', 'Mumbai', 'Jaipur']
dict_using_comp = {key:value for (key, value) in zip(state, capital)}
print("Output Dictionary using dictionary comprehensions:", dict_using_comp)

                                                Output:
            Output Dictionary using dictionary comprehensions:
    {'Rajasthan': 'Jaipur', 'Maharashtra': 'Mumbai', 'Gujarat': 'Gandhinagar'}
```

## 11.5 Set Comprehensions

Set comprehensions are pretty similar to list comprehensions. The only difference between them is that set comprehensions use curly brackets { }. Let's look at the following example to understand set comprehensions.

Example #1 : Suppose we want to create an output set which contains only the even numbers that are present in the input list. Note that set will discard all the duplicate values. Let's see how we can do this using for loops and set comprehension.

```
input_list = [1, 2, 3, 4, 4, 5, 6, 6, 6, 7, 7]
output_set = set()
# Using loop for constructing output set
for var in input_list:
            if var % 2 == 0:
                        output_set.add(var)
print("Output Set using for loop:", output_set)

                                                    Output:
                        Output Set using for loop: {2, 4, 6}
```

# Using Set comprehensions for constructing output set

```
input_list = [1, 2, 3, 4, 4, 5, 6, 6, 6, 7, 7]
set_using_comp = {var for var in input_list if var % 2 == 0}
print("Output Set using set comprehensions:", set_using_comp)

                                                    Output:
                Output Set using set comprehensions: {2, 4, 6}
```

## 11.6 Generator Comprehensions:

Generator Comprehensions are very similar to list comprehensions. One difference between them is that generator comprehensions use circular brackets whereas list comprehensions use square brackets. The major difference between them is that generators don't allocate memory for the whole list. Instead, they generate each value one by one which is why they are memory efficient. Let's look at the following example to understand generator comprehension

```
input_list = [1, 2, 3, 4, 4, 5, 6, 7, 7]

output_gen = (var for var in input_list if var % 2 == 0)
print("Output values using generator comprehensions:", end = ' ')
for var in output_gen:    print(var, end = ' ')

                                                    Output:
                Output values using generator comprehensions: 2 4 4 6
```

## 11.7 Reducing Execution time in Python using List Comprehensions

Below are the Python 3 code snippets to check the execution times for the above programs,

```
import time                              # Using for loop
start = time.time()
a = [ ]
for i in range(10**7):
        if i % 2 == 0:
                a.append(i)
print("Execution time = ", time.time()-start)
# Using list comprehension
start = time.time()
a = [i for i in range(10**7) if i % 2 == 0]
print("Execution time = ", time.time()-start)


                                                    Output:
                               Execution time =  1.558159589767456
                               Execution time =  0.9690220355987549
```

Time Functions in Python | Set 1 (time(), ctime(), sleep()...)

Python has defined a module, "time" which allows us to handle various operations regarding time, its conversions and representations, which find its use in various applications in life. The beginning of time is started measuring from 1 January, 12:00 am, 1970 and this very time is termed as "epoch" in Python.

**Operations on Time :**

- time() :- This function is used to count the number of seconds elapsed since the epoch.
- gmtime(sec) :- This function returns a structure with 9 values each representing a time attribute in sequence. It converts seconds into time attributes(days, years, months etc.) till specified seconds from epoch. If no seconds are mentioned, time is calculated till present. The structure attribute table is given below.

**Index   Attributes   Values**

0      tm_year     2008

1      tm_mon      1 to 12

2      tm_mday     1 to 31

3      tm_hour     0 to 23

4      tm_min      0 to 59

5      tm_sec      0 to 61 (60 or 61 are leap-seconds)

6      tm_wday     0 to 6

7      tm_yday     1 to 366

8      tm_isdst    -1, 0, 1 where -1 means Library determines DST

```python
# Python code to demonstrate the working of time() and gmtime()
# importing "time" module for time operations
import time
# using time() to display time since epoch
print ("Seconds elapsed since the epoch are : ", end="")
print (time.time())

# using gmtime() to return the time attribute structure
print ("Time calculated acc. to given seconds is : ")
print (time.gmtime())
```

Output

Seconds elapsed since the epoch are : 1616656136.77374

Time calculated acc. to given seconds is :

time.struct_time(tm_year=2021,   tm_mon=3,   tm_mday=25, tm_hour=7, tm_min=8, tm_sec=56, tm_wday=3, tm_yday=84, tm_isdst=0)

3. asctime("time") :- This function takes a time attributed string produced by gmtime() and returns a 24 character string denoting time.

4. ctime(sec) :- This function returns a 24 character time string but takes seconds as argument and computes time till mentioned seconds. If no argument is passed, time is calculated till present.

```python
# initializing time using gmtime()
ti = time.gmtime()

# using asctime() to display time acc. to time mentioned
print ("Time calculated using asctime() is : ",end="")
print (time.asctime(ti))


# using ctime() to diplay time string using seconds
print ("Time calculated using ctime() is : ", end="")
print (time.ctime())

                                                    Output
        Time calculated using asctime() is : Thu Mar 25 07:13:41 2021
        Time calculated using ctime() is : Thu Mar 25 12:43:41 2021
```

5. sleep(sec) :- This method is used to hault the program execution for the time specified in the arguments.

```python
# Python code to demonstrate the working of sleep()

# importing "time" module for time operations
import time

# using ctime() to show present time
print ("Start Execution : ",end="")
print (time.ctime())

# using sleep() to hault execution
time.sleep(4)

# using ctime() to show present time
print ("Stop Execution : ",end="")
print (time.ctime())

                                                    Output
        Start Execution : Thu Mar 25 12:45:53 2021
```

In this tutorial, we will learn how to develop graphical user interfaces by writing some Python GUI examples using the Tkinter package. Tkinter package is shipped with Python as a standard package, so we don't need to install anything to use it. Tkinter package is a very powerful package. If you already have installed Python, you may use IDLE which is the integrated IDE that is shipped with Python, this IDE is written using Tkinter

Basic GUI Application

GUI elements and their functionality are defined in the Tkinter module. The following code demonstrates the steps in creating a UI.

## 11.8 Python GUI

• In this part, we will learn how to develop graphical user interfaces (GUI) by writing some Python GUI examples using the Tkinter package. Tkinter package is shipped with Python as a standard package, so we don't need to install anything to use it.

• Tkinter package is a very powerful package. If you already have installed Python, you may use IDLE which is the integrated IDE that is shipped with Python, this IDE is written using Tkinter

**Basic GUI Application**

GUI elements and their functionality are defined in the Tkinter module. The following code demonstrates the steps in creating a UI.

```
from tkinter import *
window=Tk()
# add widgets here
window.title('Hello Python')
window.geometry("300x200+10+20")
window.mainloop()
```

- First of all, import the TKinter module. After importing, setup the application object by calling the Tk() function.
- This will create a top-level window (root) having a frame with a title bar, control box with the minimize and close buttons, and a client area to hold other widgets.
- The geometry() method defines the width, height and coordinates of the top left corner of the frame as below (all values are in pixels):
- window.geometry("widthxheight+XPOS+YPOS")
- The application object then enters an event listening loop by calling the mainloop() method.
- The application is now constantly waiting for any event generated on the elements in it.
- The event could be text entered in a text field, a selection made from the dropdown or radio button, single/double click actions of mouse, etc.
- The application's functionality involves executing appropriate callback functions in response to a particular type of event.
- We shall discuss event handling later in this tutorial. The event loop will terminate as and when the close button on the title bar is clicked. The above code will create the following window:

Output:

All Tkinter widget classes are inherited from the Widget class. Let's add the most commonly used widgets.

**Button**

The button can be created using the Button class. The Button class constructor requires a reference to the main window and to the options.

Signature: Button(window, attributes)

You can set the following important properties to customize a button:

- text : caption of the button
- bg : background colour
- fg : foreground colour
- font : font name and size
- image : to be displayed instead of text
- command : function to be called when clicked

```python
from tkinter import *
window=Tk()

btn=Button(window, text="This is Button widget", fg='blue')
btn.place(x=80, y=100)

window.title('Hello Python')
window.geometry("300x200+10+10")
window.mainloop()
```

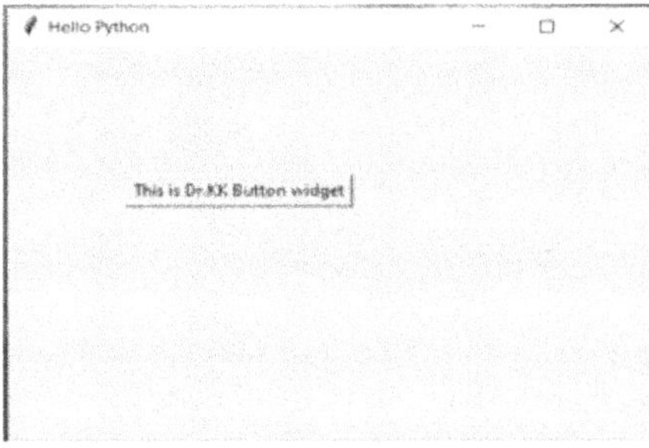

## Label

A label can be created in the GUI in Python using the Label class. The Label constructor requires the top-level window object and options parameters. Option parameters are similar to the Button object. The following adds a label in the window.

```
from tkinter import *
window=Tk()

lbl=Label(window, text="This is Label widget", fg='red', font=("Helvetica", 16))
lbl.place(x=60, y=50)
window.title('Hello Python')
window.geometry("300x200+10+10")
window.mainloop()
```

Here, the label's caption will be displayed in red colour using Helvetica font of 16 point size.

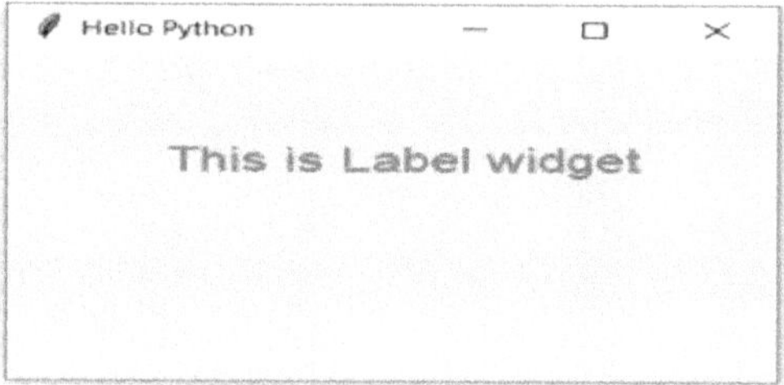


## Entry

This widget renders a single-line text box for accepting the user input. For multi-line text input use the Text widget. Apart from the properties already mentioned, the Entry class constructor accepts the following:

- bd : border size of the text box; default is 2 pixels.
- show : to convert the text box into a password field, set show property to "*".

The following code adds the text field.

txtfld=Entry(window, text="This is Entry Widget", bg='black',fg='white', bd=5)

The following example creates a window with a button, label and entry field.

```
from tkinter import *
window=Tk()

btn=Button(window, text="This is Button widget", fg='blue')
btn.place(x=80, y=100)
lbl=Label(window, text="This is Label widget", fg='red', font=("Helvetica", 16))
lbl.place(x=60, y=50)
txtfld=Entry(window, text="This is Entry Widget", bd=5)
txtfld.place(x=80, y=150)
window.title('Hello Python')
window.geometry("300x200+10+10")
window.mainloop()
```

The above example will create the following window.

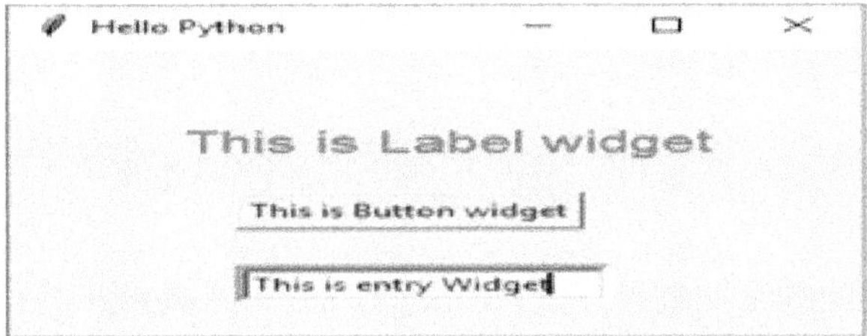


## Selection Widgets

- Radiobutton: This widget displays a toggle button having an ON/OFF state. There may be more than one button, but only one of them will be ON at a given time.
- Checkbutton: This is also a toggle button. A rectangular check box appears before its caption. Its ON state is displayed by the tick mark in the box which disappears when it is clicked to OFF.
- Combobox: This class is defined in the ttk module of tkinterpackage. It populates drop down data from a collection data type, such as a tuple or a list as values parameter.

- Listbox: Unlike Combobox, this widget displays the entire collection of string items. The user can select one or multiple items.

- The following example demonstrates the window with the selection widgets: Radiobutton, Checkbutton, Listbox and Combobox:

```python
from tkinter import *
from tkinter.ttk import Combobox
window=Tk()
var = StringVar()
var.set("one")
data=("one", "two", "three", "four")
cb=Combobox(window, values=data)
cb.place(x=60, y=150)

lb=Listbox(window, height=5, selectmode='multiple')
for num in data:
    lb.insert(END, num)
lb.place(x=250, y=150)

v0=IntVar()
v0.set(1)
r1=Radiobutton(window, text="male", variable=v0, value=1)
r2=Radiobutton(window, text="female", variable=v0, value=2)
r1.place(x=100, y=50)
r2.place(x=180, y=50)

v1 = IntVar()
v2 = IntVar()
C1 = Checkbutton(window, text = "Cricket", variable = v1)
C2 = Checkbutton(window, text = "Tennis", variable = v2)
C1.place(x=100, y=100)
C2.place(x=180, y=100)

window.title('Hello Python')
window.geometry("400x300+10+10")
window.mainloop()
```

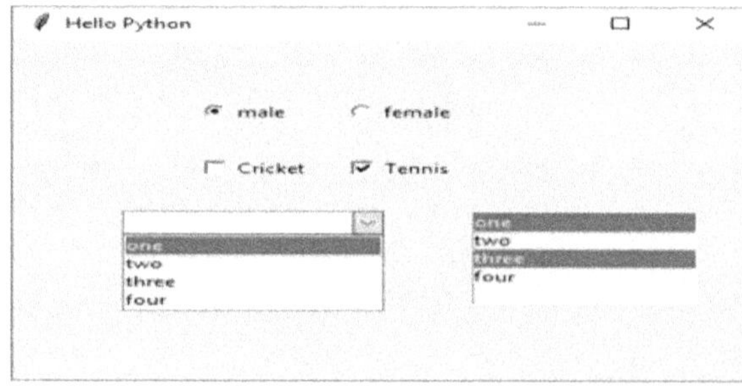

To add radio buttons, simply you can use RadioButton class like this:

```
rad1 = Radiobutton(window, text='First', value=1)
```

Note that you should set the value for every radio button with a different value, otherwise, they won't work.

```
from tkinter import *
from tkinter.ttk import *
window = Tk()
window.title("Welcome to LikeGeeks app")
window.geometry('350x200')
rad1 = Radiobutton(window,text='First', value=1)
rad2 = Radiobutton(window,text='Second', value=2)
rad3 = Radiobutton(window,text='Third', value=3)
rad1.grid(column=0, row=0)
rad2.grid(column=1, row=0)
rad3.grid(column=2, row=0)
window.mainloop()
```

The result of the above code looks like this:

Also, you can set the command of any of these radio buttons to a specific function, so if the user clicks on any one of them, it runs the function code.

This is an example:

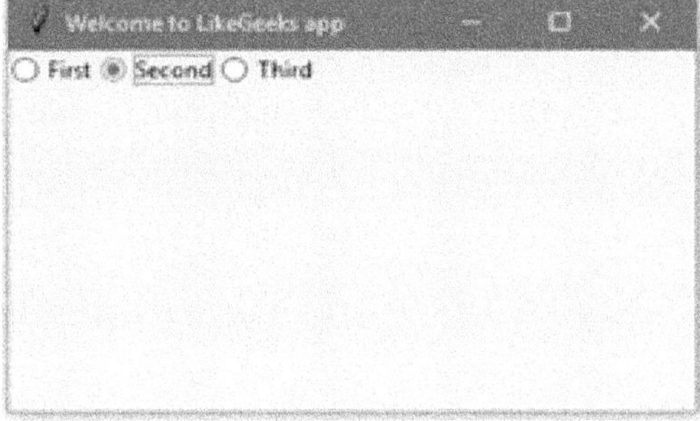

Get radio button value (selected radio button)

To get the currently selected radio button or the radio button value, you can pass the variable parameter to the radio buttons, and later you can get its value.

```python
from tkinter import *
from tkinter.ttk import *
window = Tk()
window.title("Welcome to KARTHEEBAN DENO")
selected = IntVar()
rad1 = Radiobutton(window, text='First', value=1, variable=selected)
rad2 = Radiobutton(window, text='Second', value=2, variable=selected)
rad3 = Radiobutton(window, text='Third', value=3, variable=selected)

def clicked():
   print(selected.get())

btn = Button(window, text="Click Me", command=clicked)
rad1.grid(column=0, row=0)
rad2.grid(column=1, row=0)
rad3.grid(column=2, row=0)
btn.grid(column=3, row=0)
window.mainloop()
```

Output

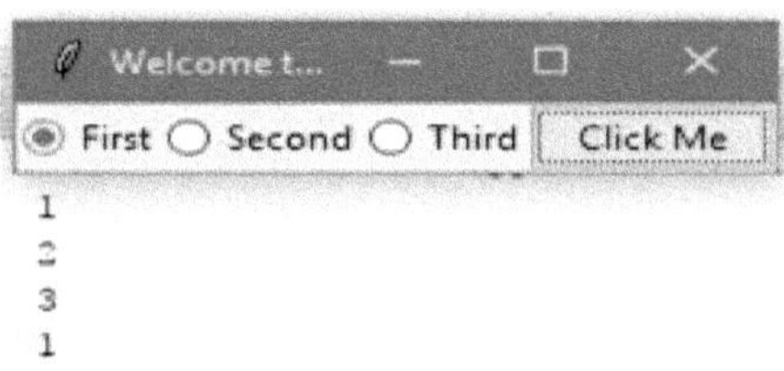


Every time you select a radio button, the value of the variable will be changed to the value of the selected radio button.

**Create a MessageBox**

To show a message box using Tkinter, you can use the messagebox library like this:

```
from tkinter import messagebox
messagebox.showinfo('Message title', 'Message content')
```

Let's show a message box when the user clicks a button.

```
from tkinter import *
from tkinter import messagebox
window = Tk()
window.title("Welcome to LikeGeeks app")
window.geometry('350x200')

def clicked():
    messagebox.showinfo('Message title', 'Message content')
btn = Button(window,text='Click here', command=clicked)
btn.grid(column=0,row=0)
window.mainloop()
```

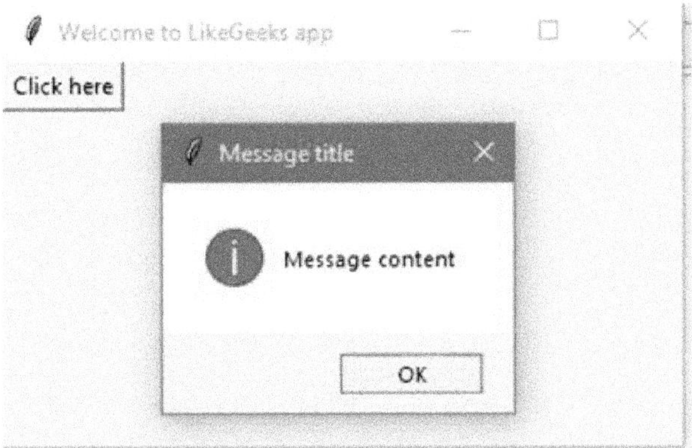


When you click the button, an info message box will appear.

**Event Handling**

An event is a notification received by the application object from various GUI widgets as a result of user interaction. The Application object is always anticipating events as it runs an event listening loop. User's actions include mouse button click or double click, keyboard key pressed while control is inside the text box, certain element gains or goes out of focus etc. Events are expressed as strings in <modifier-type-qualifier> format.

Many events are represented just as qualifier. The type defines the class of the event. The following table shows how the Tkinter recognizes different events:

| Event | Modifier | Type | Qualifier | Action |
|---|---|---|---|---|
| <Button-1> | | Button | 1 | Left mouse button click. |
| <Button-2> | | Button | 2 | Middle mouse button click. |
| <Destroy> | | Destroy | | Window is being destroyed. |
| <Double-Button-1> | Double | Button | 1 | Double-click first mouse button 1. |
| <Enter> | Enter | | | Cursor enters window. |
| <Expose> | | Expose | | Window fully or partially exposed. |
| <KeyPress-a> | | KeyPress | a | Any key has been pressed. |
| <KeyRelease> | | KeyRelease | | Any key has been released. |
| <Leave> | | Leave | | Cursor leaves window. |
| <Print> | | | Print | PRINT key has been pressed. |
| <FocusIn> | | FocusIn | | Widget gains focus. |
| <FocusOut> | | FocusOut | | widget loses focus. |

An event should be registered with one or more GUI widgets in the application. If it's not, it will be ignored. In Tkinter, there are two ways to register an event with a widget. First way is by using the bind() method and the second way is by using the command parameter in the widget constructor.

## Bind() Method

The bind() method associates an event to a callback function so that, when the even occurs, the function is called.  Syntax:

Widget.bind(event, callback)

For example, to invoke the MyButtonClicked() function on left button click, use the following code:

Example: Even Binding

```
from tkinter import *
window=Tk()
btn = Button(window, text='OK')
btn.bind('<Button-1>', MyButtonClicked)
```

The event object is characterized by many properties such as source widget, position coordinates, mouse button number and event type. These can be passed to the callback function if required.

## Command Parameter

Each widget primarily responds to a particular type. For example, Button is a source of the Button event. So, it is by default bound to it. Constructor methods of many widget classes have an optional parameter called command. This command parameter is set to callback the function which will be invoked whenever its bound event occurs. This method is more convenient than the bind() method. btn = Button(window, text='OK', command=myEventHandlerFunction). In the example given below, the application window has two text input fields and another one to display the result. There are two button objects with the captions Add and Subtract. The user is expected to enter the number in the two Entry widgets. Their addition or subtraction is displayed in the third. The first button (Add) is configured using the command parameter. Its value is the add() method in the class. The second button uses the bind() method to register the left button click with the sub() method. Both methods read the contents of the text fields by the get() method of the Entry widget, parse to numbers, perform the addition/subtraction and display the result in third text field using the insert() method.

Example

```python
from tkinter import *
class MyWindow:
    def __init__(self, win):
        self.lbl1=Label(win, text='First number')
        self.lbl2=Label(win, text='Second number')
        self.lbl3=Label(win, text='Result')
        self.t1=Entry(bd=3)
        self.t2=Entry()
        self.t3=Entry()
        self.btn1 = Button(win, text='Add')
        self.btn2=Button(win, text='Subtract')
        self.lbl1.place(x=100, y=50)
        self.t1.place(x=200, y=50)
        self.lbl2.place(x=100, y=100)
        self.t2.place(x=200, y=100)
        self.b1=Button(win, text='Add', command=self.add)
        self.b2=Button(win, text='Subtract')
        self.b2.bind('<Button-1>', self.sub)
        self.b1.place(x=100, y=150)
        self.b2.place(x=200, y=150)
        self.lbl3.place(x=100, y=200)
        self.t3.place(x=200, y=200)
    def add(self):
        self.t3.delete(0, 'end')
        num1=int(self.t1.get())
        num2=int(self.t2.get())
        result=num1+num2
        self.t3.insert(END, str(result))
    def sub(self, event):
        self.t3.delete(0, 'end')
        num1=int(self.t1.get())
        num2=int(self.t2.get())
        result=num1-num2
        self.t3.insert(END, str(result))
window=Tk()
mywin=MyWindow(window)
window.title('Hello Python')
window.geometry("400x300+10+10")
window.mainloop()
```

The above example creates the following UI.

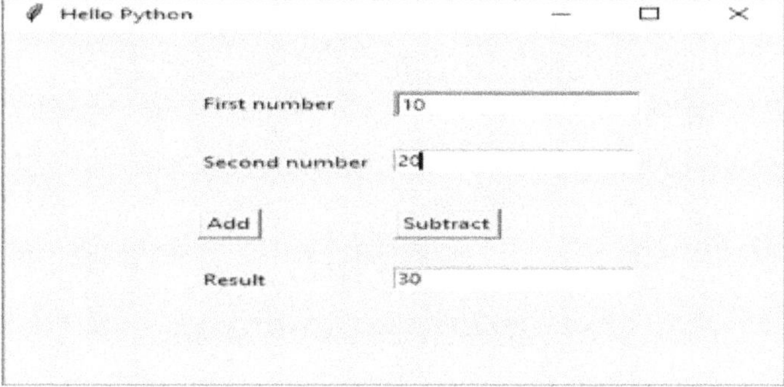

Thus, you can create the UI using TKinter in Python.

**Python - Tkinter pack() Method**

This geometry manager organizes widgets in blocks before placing them in the parent widget

Syntax

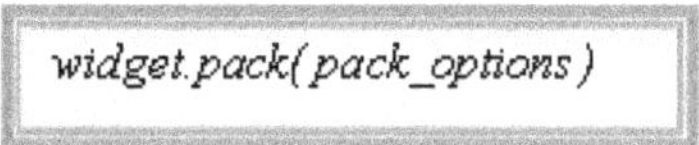

Here is the list of possible options −

- expand − When set to true, widget expands to fill any space not otherwise used in widget's parent.
- fill − Determines whether widget fills any extra space allocated to it by the packer, or keeps its own minimal dimensions: NONE (default), X (fill only horizontally), Y (fill only vertically), or BOTH (fill both horizontally and vertically).
- side − Determines which side of the parent widget packs against: TOP (default), BOTTOM, LEFT, or RIGHT.

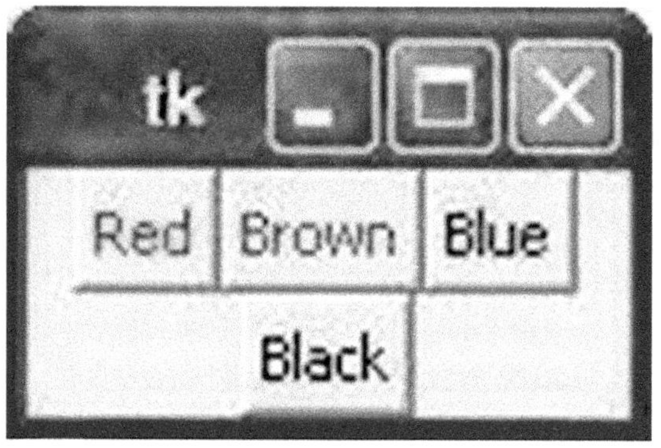

```
from Tkinter import *
root = Tk()
frame = Frame(root)
frame.pack()
bottomframe = Frame(root)
bottomframe.pack( side = BOTTOM )
redbutton = Button(frame, text="Red", fg="red")
redbutton.pack( side = LEFT)
greenbutton = Button(frame, text="green", fg="green")
greenbutton.pack( side = LEFT )
bluebutton = Button(frame, text="Blue", fg="blue")
bluebutton.pack( side = LEFT )
blackbutton = Button(bottomframe, text="Black", fg="black")
blackbutton.pack( side = BOTTOM)
root.mainloop()
```

Code #1: Putting a widget inside frame and filling entire frame. We can do this with the help of expand and fill options.

```
# Importing tkinter module
from tkinter import * from tkinter.ttk import *

# creating Tk window
master = Tk()

# cretaing a Fra, e which can expand according
# to the size of the window
pane = Frame(master)
pane.pack(fill = BOTH, expand = True)

# button widgets which can also expand and fill
# in the parent widget entirely
# Button 1
b1 = Button(pane, text = "Click me !")
b1.pack(fill = BOTH, expand = True)

# Button 2
b2 = Button(pane, text = "Click me too")
b2.pack(fill = BOTH, expand = True)

# Execute Tkinter
master.mainloop()
```

Output

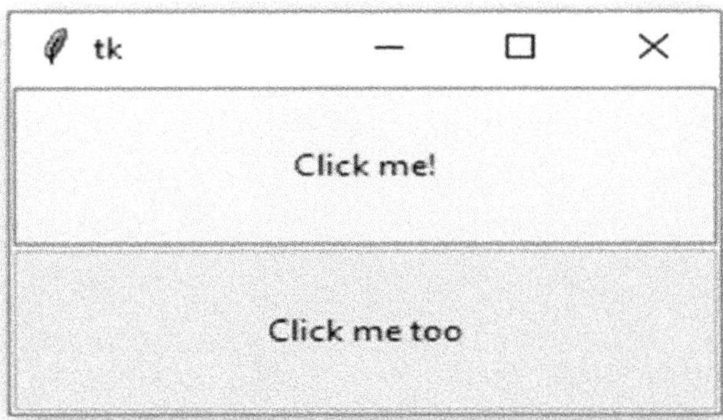


 Code #2: Placing widgets on top of each other and side by side.
We can do this by side option.

```python
# Importing tkinter module
from tkinter import *
# from tkinter.ttk import *

# creating Tk window
master = Tk()

# cretaing a Fra, e which can expand according
# to the size of the window
pane = Frame(master)
pane.pack(fill = BOTH, expand = True)

# button widgets which can also expand and fill
# in the parent widget entirely
# Button 1
b1 = Button(pane, text = "Click me !",
                        background = "red", fg = "white")
b1.pack(side = TOP, expand = True, fill = BOTH)

# Button 2
b2 = Button(pane, text = "Click me too",
                        background = "blue", fg = "white")
b2.pack(side = TOP, expand = True, fill = BOTH)

# Button 3
b3 = Button(pane, text = "I'm also button",
                        background = "green", fg = "white")
b3.pack(side = TOP, expand = True, fill = BOTH)

# Execute Tkinter
master.mainloop()
```

Output

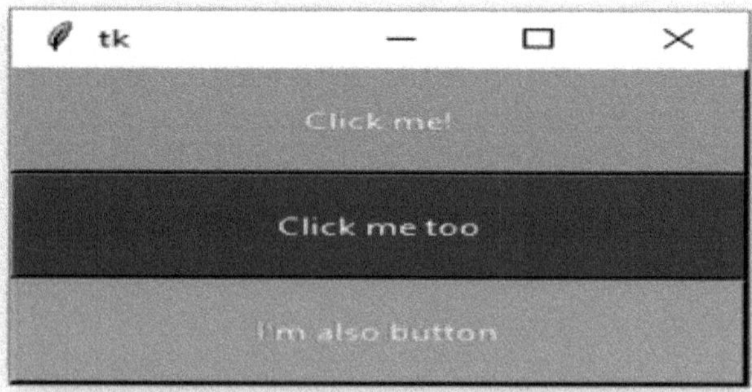

```python
# Importing tkinter module
from tkinter import *
# from tkinter.ttk import *

# creating Tk window
master = Tk()

# cretaing a Fra, e which can expand according
# to the size of the window
pane = Frame(master)
pane.pack(fill = BOTH, expand = True)
# button widgets which can also expand and fill
# in the parent widget entirely
# Button 1
b1 = Button(pane, text = "Click me !",
                        background = "red", fg = "white")
b1.pack(side = LEFT, expand = True, fill = BOTH)
# Button 2
b2 = Button(pane, text = "Click me too",
                        background = "blue", fg = "white")
b2.pack(side = LEFT, expand = True, fill = BOTH)
# Button 3
b3 = Button(pane, text = "I'm also button",
                        background = "green", fg = "white")
b3.pack(side = LEFT, expand = True, fill = BOTH)

# Execute Tkinter
master.mainloop()
```

Output

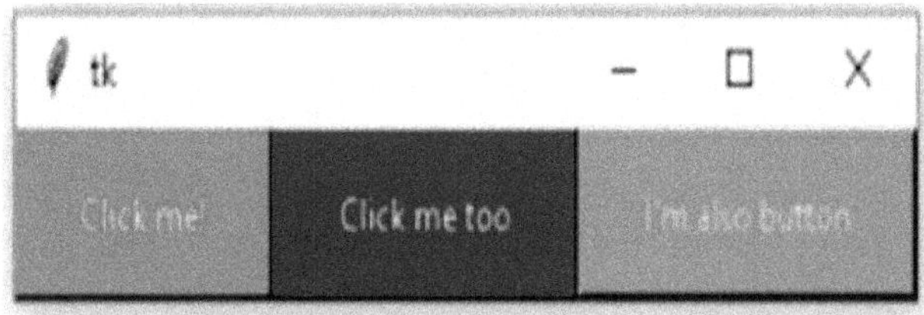

**Add a Progressbar widget**

To create a progress bar, you can use the progressbar class like this:

```python
from tkinter.ttk import Progressbar
bar = Progressbar(window, length=200)
```

You can set the progress bar value like this:

```python
bar['value'] = 70
```

You can set this value based on any process you want like downloading a file or completing a task.

**Change Progressbar color**

Changing Progressbar color is a bit tricky, but super easy. First, we will create a style and set the background color and finally set the created style to the Progressbar.

```python
from tkinter import *
from tkinter.ttk import Progressbar
from tkinter import ttk
window = Tk()
window.title("Welcome to LikeGeeks app")
window.geometry('350x200')
style = ttk.Style()
style.theme_use('default')
style.configure("black.Horizontal.TProgressbar", background='black')
bar = Progressbar(window, length=200, style='black.Horizontal.TProgressbar')
bar['value'] = 70
bar.grid(column=0, row=0)
window.mainloop()
```

And the result will be like this:

Add a ScrolledText widget (Tkinter textarea)

To add a ScrolledText widget, you can use the ScrolledText class like this:

```
from tkinter import scrolledtext
txt = scrolledtext.ScrolledText(window,width=40,height=10)
```

Here we specify the width and the height of the ScrolledText widget, otherwise, it will fill the entire window.

```
from tkinter import *
from tkinter import scrolledtext
window = Tk()
window.title("Welcome to Python GUI Programming")
window.geometry('350x200')
txt = scrolledtext.ScrolledText(window,width=40,height=10)
txt.grid(column=0,row=0)
window.mainloop()
```

The result as you can see:

Python - Tkinter Scrollbar

This widget provides a slide controller that is used to implement vertical scrolled widgets, such as Listbox, Text and Canvas. Note that you can also create horizontal scrollbars on Entry widgets.

Syntax

```
w = Scrollbar ( master, option, ... )
```

Parameters

- master − This represents the parent window.
- options − Here is the list of most commonly used options for this widget. These options can be used as key-value pairs separated by commas.

## Methods

Scrollbar objects have these methods −

- get() -Returns two numbers (a, b) describing the current position of the slider. The a value gives the position of the left or top edge of the slider, for horizontal and vertical scrollbars respectively; the b value gives the position of the right or bottom edge.
- set(first, last) -To connect a scrollbar to another widget w, set w's xscrollcommand or yscrollcommand to the scrollbar's set() method. The arguments have the same meaning as the values returned by the get() method.

```
from Tkinter import *

root = Tk()
scrollbar = Scrollbar(root)
scrollbar.pack( side = RIGHT, fill = Y )

mylist = Listbox(root, yscrollcommand = scrollbar.set )
for line in range(100):
    mylist.insert(END, "This is line number " + str(line))

mylist.pack( side = LEFT, fill = BOTH )
scrollbar.config( command = mylist.yview )

mainloop()
```

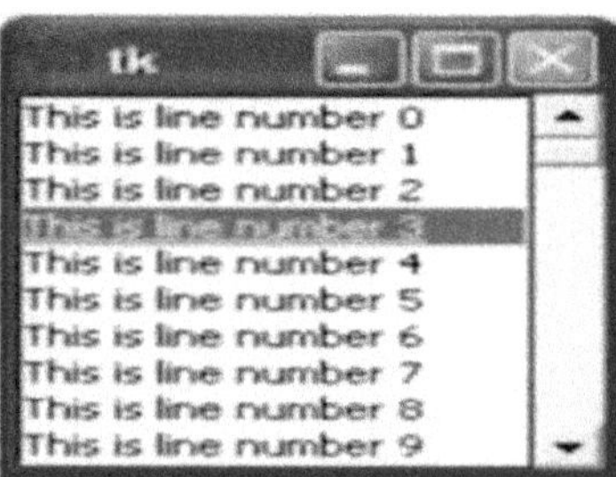

**Python - Tkinter Menu**

The goal of this widget is to allow us to create all kinds of menus that can be used by our applications. The core functionality provides ways to create three menu types: pop-up, toplevel and pull-down.

It is also possible to use other extended widgets to implement new types of menus, such as the OptionMenu widget, which implements a special type that generates a pop-up list of items within a selection.

Syntax:

```
w = Menu ( master, option, ... )
```

Parameters

- master − This represents the parent window.
- options − Here is the list of most commonly used options for this widget. These options can be used as key-value pairs separated by commas.

1. Activebackground - The background color that will appear on a choice when it is under the mouse.
2. Activeborderwidth - Specifies the width of a border drawn around a choice when it is under the mouse. Default is 1 pixel.
3. Activeforeground- The foreground color that will appear on a choice when it is under the mouse.
4. Bg-The background color for choices not under the mouse.
5. Bd- The width of the border around all the choices. Default is 1.
6. Cursor - The cursor that appears when the mouse is over the choices, but only when the menu has been torn off.
7. Disabledforeground - The color of the text for items whose state is DISABLED.
8. Font - The default font for textual choices.

9. Fg-The foreground color used for choices not under the mouse.

10. Postcommand -You can set this option to a procedure, and that procedure will be called every time someone brings up this menu.

11. Relief -The default 3-D effect for menus is relief=RAISED.

12. Image-To display an image on this menubutton.

13. Selectcolor-Specifies the color displayed in checkbuttons and radiobuttons when they are selected.

14. Tearoff-Normally, a menu can be torn off, the first position (position 0) in the list of choices is occupied by the tear-off element, and the additional choices are added starting at position 1. If you set tearoff=0, the menu will not have a tear-off feature, and choices will be added starting at position 0.

15. Title-Normally, the title of a tear-off menu window will be the same as the text of the menubutton or cascade that lead to this menu. If you want to change the title of that window, set the title option to that string.

## Methods

These methods are available on Menu objects −

1  add_command (options) -Adds a menu item to the menu.

2  add_radiobutton( options )-Creates a radio button menu item.

3  add_checkbutton( options )-Creates a check button menu item.

4  add_cascade(options)-Creates a new hierarchical menu by associating a given menu to a parent menu

5  add_separator()-Adds a separator line to the menu.

6  add( type, options )-Adds a specific type of menu item to the menu.

7  delete( startindex [, endindex ])-Deletes the menu items ranging from startindex to endindex.

8  entryconfig( index, options )-Allows you to modify a menu item, which is identified by the index, and change its options.

9  index(item)-Returns the index number of the given menu item label.

10  insert_separator ( index )-Insert a new separator at the position specified by index.

11  invoke ( index )-Calls the command callback associated with the choice at position index. If a checkbutton, its state is toggled between set and cleared; if a radiobutton, that choice is set.

Example

```
from tkinter import *
from tkinter import Menu
window = Tk()

window.title("Welcome to LikeGeeks app")

menu = Menu(window)

new_item = Menu(menu)

new_item.add_command(label='New')

menu.add_cascade(label='File', menu=new_item)

window.config(menu=menu)

window.mainloop()
```

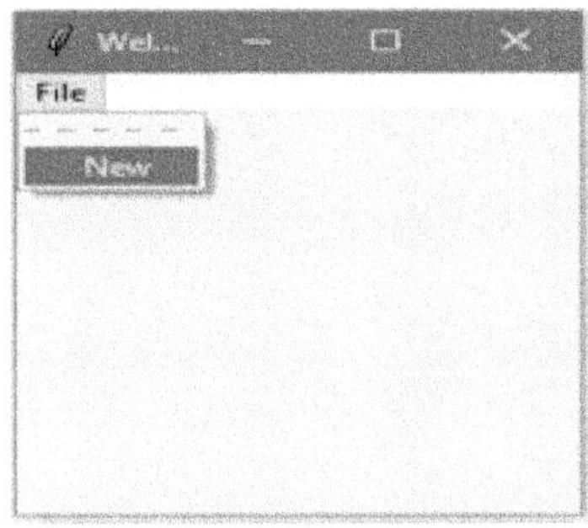

## Example 2

```python
from Tkinter import *
def donothing():
    filewin = Toplevel(root)
    button = Button(filewin, text="Do nothing button")
    button.pack()
root = Tk()
menubar = Menu(root)
filemenu = Menu(menubar, tearoff=0)
filemenu.add_command(label="New", command=donothing)
filemenu.add_command(label="Open", command=donothing)
filemenu.add_command(label="Save", command=donothing)
filemenu.add_command(label="Save as...", command=donothing)
filemenu.add_command(label="Close", command=donothing)

filemenu.add_separator()
filemenu.add_command(label="Exit", command=root.quit)
menubar.add_cascade(label="File", menu=filemenu)
editmenu = Menu(menubar, tearoff=0)
editmenu.add_command(label="Undo", command=donothing)
editmenu.add_separator()
editmenu.add_command(label="Cut", command=donothing)
editmenu.add_command(label="Copy", command=donothing)
editmenu.add_command(label="Paste", command=donothing)
editmenu.add_command(label="Delete", command=donothing)
editmenu.add_command(label="Select All", command=donothing)
menubar.add_cascade(label="Edit", menu=editmenu)
helpmenu = Menu(menubar, tearoff=0)
helpmenu.add_command(label="Help Index", command=donothing)
helpmenu.add_command(label="About...", command=donothing)
menubar.add_cascade(label="Help", menu=helpmenu)
```

## Output

When the above code is executed, it produces the following result

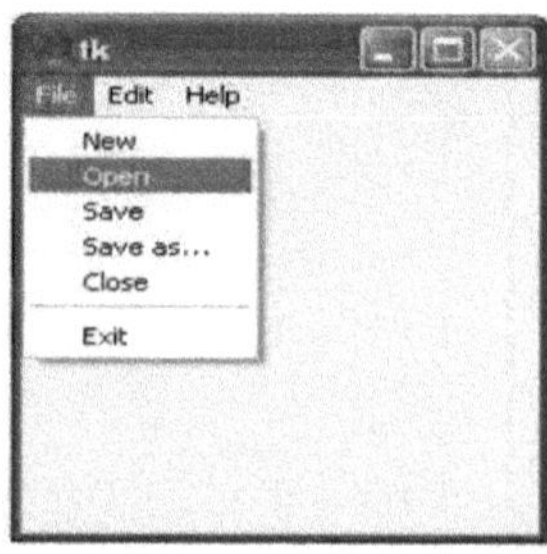

Using this way, you can add many menu items as you want.

Example 3:

```python
from tkinter import *
from tkinter import Menu

window = Tk()

window.title("Welcome to Dr. KK Menu Programs")
menu = Menu(window)
new_item = Menu(menu)
new_item.add_command(label='New')
new_item.add_separator()
new_item.add_command(label='Edit')
menu.add_cascade(label='File', menu=new_item)
window.config(menu=menu)
window.mainloop()
```

Output

You may notice a dashed line at the beginning, well, if you click that line, it will show the menu items in a small separate window. You can disable this feature by disabling the tearoff feature like this:

new_item = Menu(menu, tearoff=0)

## 11.9 Tkinter Toplevel

- The Toplevel widget is used to create and display the toplevel windows which are directly managed by the window manager.
- The toplevel widget may or may not have the parent window on the top of them.
- The toplevel widget is used when a python application needs to represent some extra
- information, pop-up, or the group of widgets on the new window.
- The toplevel windows have the title bars, borders, and other window decorations.
- The syntax to use the Toplevel widget is given below.

A List of possible options is given below.

| SN | Options | Description |
|----|---------|-------------|
| 1 | bg | It represents the background color of the window. |
| 2 | bd | It represents the border size of the window. |
| 3 | cursor | The mouse pointer is changed to the cursor type set to the arrow, dot, etc. when the mouse is in the window. |
| 4 | class_ | The text selected in the text widget is exported to be selected to the window manager. We can set this to 0 to make this behavior false. |
| 5 | font | The font type of the text inserted into the widget. |
| 6 | fg | The foreground color of the widget. |
| 7 | height | It represents the height of the window. |
| 8 | relief | It represents the type of the window. |
| 9 | width | It represents the width of the window, |

## Specialized Sorts

Sorting any sequence is very easy in Python using built-in method sorted() which does all the hard work for you. Sorted() sorts any sequence (list, tuple) and always returns a list with the elements in sorted manner, without modifying the original sequence.

*Syntax : sorted(iterable, key, reverse)*

Parameters : sorted takes three parameters from which two are optional.

- Iterable : sequence (list, tuple, string) or collection (dictionary, set, frozenset) or any other iterator that needs to be sorted.
- Key(optional) : A function that would server as a key or a basis of sort comparison.
- Reverse(optional) : If set true, then the iterable would be sorted in reverse (descending) order, by default it is set as false.

```
x = [2, 8, 1, 4, 6, 3, 7]
print ("Sorted List returned : "),
print (sorted(x))
print ("\nReverse sort : "),
print (sorted(x, reverse = True))
print ("\nOriginal list not modified : "),
print (x)
                                              Output :
                         Sorted List returned : [1, 2, 3, 4, 6, 7, 8]
                                Reverse sort : [8, 7, 6, 4, 3, 2, 1]
                     Original list not modified : [2, 8, 1, 4, 6, 3, 7]
```

Example 2:

```
x = ['q', 'w', 'r', 'e', 't', 'y']
print (sorted(x))
x = ('q', 'w', 'e', 'r', 't', 'y')
print (sorted(x))
x = "python"
print (sorted(x))
x = {'q': 1, 'w': 2, 'e': 3, 'r': 4, 't': 5, 'y': 6}
print (sorted(x))
x = {'q', 'w', 'e', 'r', 't', 'y'}
print (sorted(x))
x = frozenset(('q', 'w', 'e', 'r', 't', 'y'))
print (sorted(x))
```

Output :

['e', 'q', 'r', 't', 'w', 'y']
['e', 'q', 'r', 't', 'w', 'y']
['h', 'n', 'o', 'p', 't', 'y']
['e', 'q', 'r', 't', 'w', 'y']
['e', 'q', 'r', 't', 'w', 'y']
['e', 'q', 'r', 't', 'w', 'y']


**Custom Sorting using the key parameter**


sorted() function has an optional parameter called 'key' which takes a function as its value. This key function transforms each element before sorting, it takes the value and returns 1 value which is then used within sort instead of the original value. For example, if we pass a list of strings in sorted(), it gets sorted alphabetically . But if we specify key = len, i.e. give len function as key, then the strings would be passed to len, and the value it returns, i.e. the length of strings will be sorted. Which means that the strings would be sorted based on their lengths instead

Example 1:

```
L = ["cccc", "b", "dd", "aaa"]

print ("Normal sort :", sorted(L))

print ("Sort with len :", sorted(L, key = len))
```

Output :

Normal sort : ['aaa', 'b', 'cccc', 'dd']

Sort with len : ['b', 'dd', 'aaa', 'cccc']

Example 2:

```
# Sort a list of integers based on
# their remainder on dividing from 7

def func(x):
        return x % 7

L = [15, 3, 11, 7]

print ("Normal sort :", sorted(L))
print ("Sorted with key:", sorted(L, key = func))
```

Output :

Normal sort : [3, 7, 11, 15]
Sorted with key: [7, 15, 3, 11]

# CHAPTER XII

# Data Structures and GUI, CGI Scripts

## 12.1 Matplotlib – Introduction

Human minds are more understandable to represent data using graph rather than textual data. We can easily understand and take better decision after analyzing visual representation of the data using graphs. In python, Matplotlib is an important open-source drawing library tool for generating different types of visualization reports like line plots, scatter plots, histograms, bar charts, pie charts, box plots, and many more different plots with small lines of code. Using this library, it is possible to draw 3-dimensional plotting. Overall, this Matplotlib library in python used to create static, interactive and animated visualizations in Python.

The matplotlib library for Python contains many sub-modules. One such important module is Pyplot. This Pyplot is a library consisting of a collection of functions/methods used for plotting simple 2D graphs using Python. Pyplot can be imported using import matplotlib.

## 12.2 Environment Setup for Matplotlib

Matplotlib is an overall package for creating static, animated, and interactive visualizations in Python. It literally opens up a whole new world of possibilities for you! Especially when it is used with Numpy or Pandas library, one can do unimaginable things. The plots give may give a new insight altogether. Now, the question arises i.e. How to make it running on your computer? But a more primary question would be, what are its pre-requisites or as we call it, dependencies for the software to run on your computer?

Dependencies

- Python (>= 3.6)
- FreeType (>= 2.3)
- libpng (>= 1.2)

- NumPy (>= 1.11)
- setuptools
- cycler (>= 0.10.0)
- dateutil (>= 2.1)
- kiwisolver (>= 1.0.0)
- pyparsing

## 12.3 Python Matplotlib

There are various plots can be created using python matplotlib such as line plots, scatter plots, histograms, bar charts, pie charts, box plots. Consider the following code to generate the simple graph using matplotlib in python. The various plots we can utilize using Pyplot are Line Plot, Histogram, Scatter, 3D Plot, Image, Contour, and Polar.

Example 1:

```
import matplotlib.pyplot as plt

x= [1,2,3,4,5]
y= [2,4,6,8,10]
plt.plot(x,y)
plt.show()
```

Output:

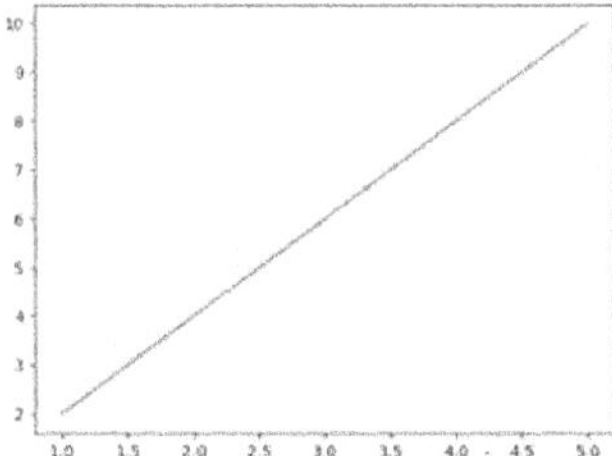

Example 2:

```
import matplotlib.pyplot as plt
x = [10, 20, 30, 40]              # initializing the data
y = [20, 30, 40, 50]
plt.plot(x, y)                    # plotting the data
# Adding the title
```

```
plt.title("Simple Plot")
# Adding the labels
plt.ylabel("y-axis")
plt.xlabel("x-axis")
plt.show()
```

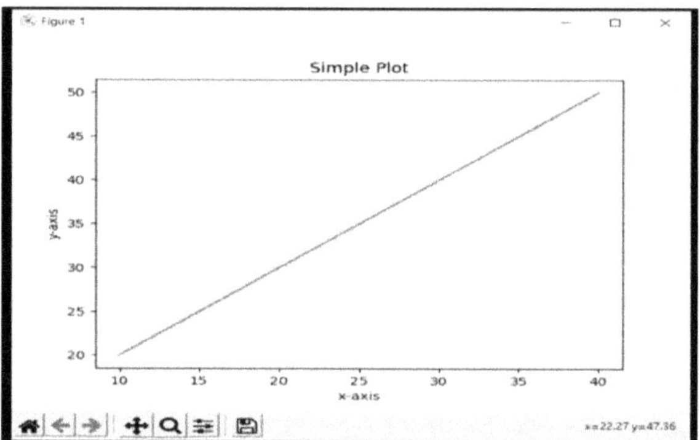

In the above example, the elements of X and Y provides the coordinates for the x axis and y axis and a straight line is plotted against those coordinates.

Example3;

```
# importing the required module
import matplotlib.pyplot as plt

# x axis values
x = [1, 2, 3]
# corresponding y axis values
y = [2, 4, 1]

# plotting the points
plt.plot(x, y)

# naming the x axis
plt.xlabel('x - axis')
# naming the y axis
plt.ylabel('y - axis')

# giving a title to my graph
plt.title('My first graph!')

# function to show the plot
plt.show()
```

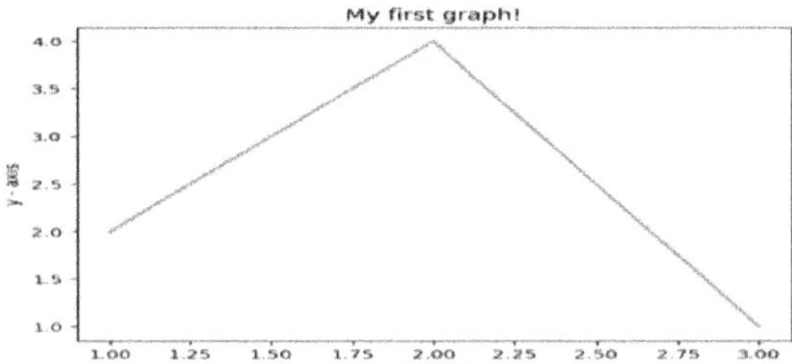

The code seems self explanatory. Following steps were followed:

- Define the x-axis and corresponding y-axis values as lists.
- Plot them on canvas using .plot() function.
- Give a name to x-axis and y-axis using .xlabel() and .ylabel() functions.
- Give a title to your plot using .title() function.
- Finally, to view your plot, we use .show() function.

**Plotting two or more lines on same plot**

Example4:

```python
import matplotlib.pyplot as plt
# line 1 points
x1 = [1, 2, 3]
y1 = [2, 4, 1]
# plotting the line 1 points
plt.plot(x1, y1, label = "line 1")
# line 2 points
x2 = [1, 2, 3]
y2 = [4, 1, 3]
# plotting the line 2 points
plt.plot(x2, y2, label = "line 2")
# naming the x axis
plt.xlabel('x - axis')
# naming the y axis
plt.ylabel('y - axis')
# giving a title to my graph
plt.title('Two lines on same graph!')

# show a legend on the plot
plt.legend()

# function to show the plot
plt.show()
```

Output:

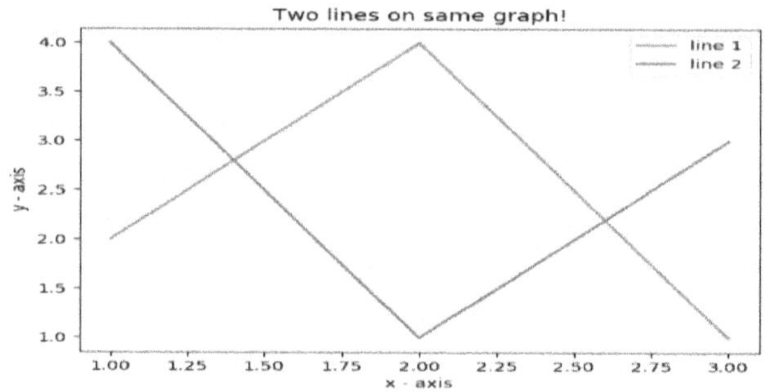


- Here, we plot two lines on same graph. We differentiate between them by giving them a name(label) which is passed as an argument of .plot() function.
- The small rectangular box giving information about type of line and its color is called legend. We can add a legend to our plot using .legend() function.

## 12.4 Customization of Plots

Here, we discuss some elementary customizations applicable on almost any plot.

```python
import matplotlib.pyplot as plt

# x axis values
x = [1,2,3,4,5,6]
# corresponding y axis values
y = [2,4,1,5,2,6]

# plotting the points
plt.plot(x, y, color='green', linestyle='dashed', linewidth = 3,
         marker='o', markerfacecolor='blue', markersize=12)

# setting x and y axis range
plt.ylim(1, 8)
plt.xlim(1, 8)

# naming the x axis
plt.xlabel('x - axis')
# naming the y axis
plt.ylabel('y - axis')
# giving a title to my graph
plt.title('Some cool customizations!')

# function to show the plot
plt.show()
```

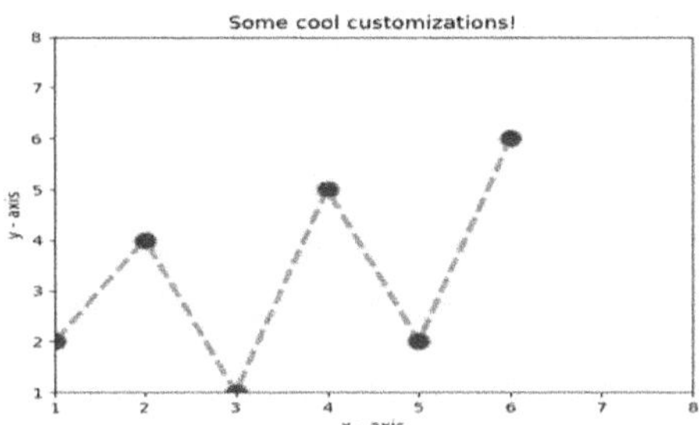

## Example 6:

```python
# Python Program to illustrate Linear Plotting

import matplotlib.pyplot as plt

# year contains the x-axis values and e-india & e-bangladesh are the y-axis values for //plotting
year = [1972, 1982, 1992, 2002, 2012]
e_india = [100.6, 158.61, 305.54, 394.96, 724.79]
e_bangladesh = [10.5, 25.21, 58.65, 119.27, 274.87]

# plotting of x-axis(year) and y-axis(power consumption)
# with different colored labels of two countries

plt.plot(year, e_india, color = 'orange', label = 'India')

plt.plot(year, e_bangladesh, color = 'g', label = 'Bangladesh')

# naming of x-axis and y-axis
plt.xlabel('Years')
plt.ylabel('Power consumption in kWh')

# naming the title of the plot
plt.title('Electricity consumption per capita\
of India and Bangladesh')

plt.legend()
plt.show()
```

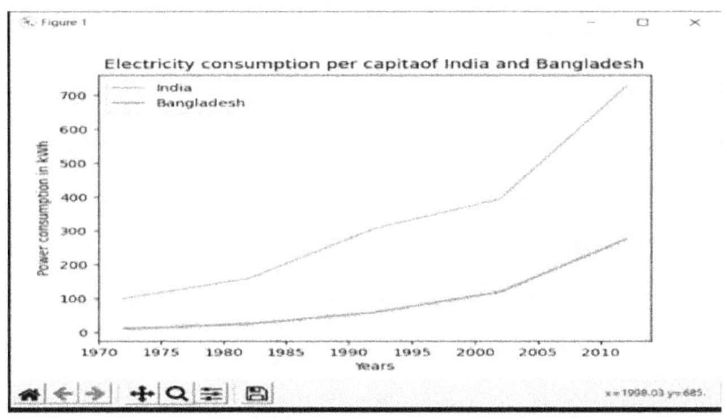

Example 7:

```python
# Python Program to illustrate Linear Plotting
import matplotlib.pyplot as plt

year = [1972, 1982, 1992, 2002, 2012]
e_india = [100.6, 158.61, 305.54,
                394.96, 724.79]

e_bangladesh = [10.5, 25.21, 58.65,
                        119.27, 274.87]


# formatting of line style and
# plotting of co-ordinates
plt.plot(year, e_india, color='orange',
                marker='o', markersize=12,
                label='India')

plt.plot(year, e_bangladesh, color='g',
                linestyle='dashed', linewidth=2,
                label='Bangladesh')
plt.xlabel('Years')
plt.ylabel('Power consumption in kWh')

plt.title('Electricity consumption per capita of India and Bangladesh')
plt.legend()
plt.show()
```

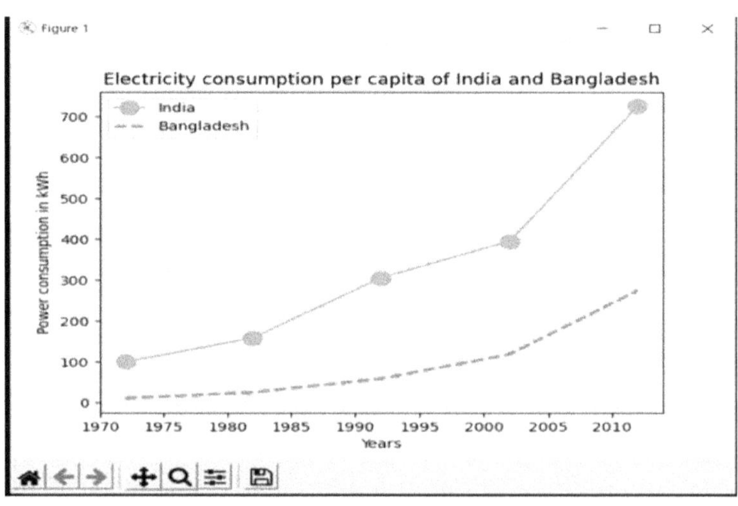

## 12.5 Bar Chart

Bar graphs are one of the most common types of graphs and are used to show data associated with the categorical variables. Matplotlib provides a bar() to make bar graphs which accepts arguments such as: categorical variables, their value and color.

Example1:

```python
from matplotlib import pyplot as plt
players = ['Virat', 'Rohit', 'Shikhar', 'Hardik']
runs = [51, 87, 45, 67]
plt.bar(players, runs, color = 'green')
plt.title('Score Card')
plt.xlabel('Players')
plt.ylabel('Runs')
plt.show()
```

Output

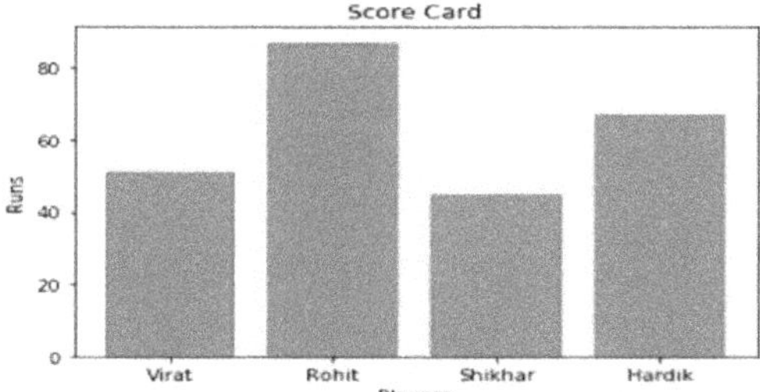

Another function barh() is used to make horizontal bar graphs. It accepts xerr or yerr as arguments (in case of vertical graphs) to depict the variance in our data as follows:

```python
from matplotlib import pyplot as plt
players = ['Virat', 'Rohit', 'Shikhar', 'Hardik']
runs = [51, 87, 45, 67]
plt.barh(players, runs, color = 'green')
plt.title('Score Card')
plt.xlabel('Players')
plt.ylabel('Runs')
plt.show()
```

# Output

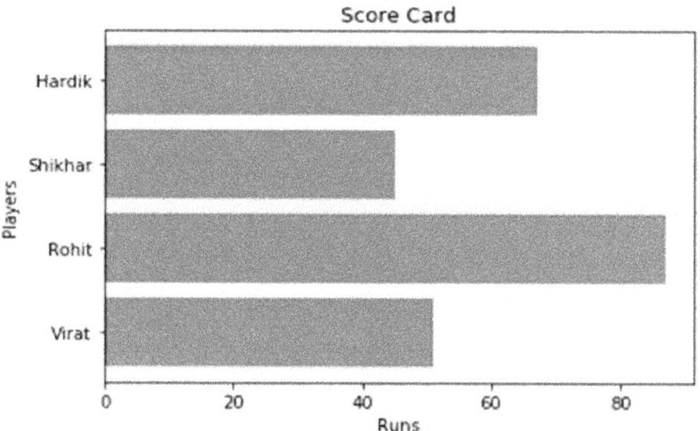



```
import matplotlib.pyplot as plt

# x-coordinates of left sides of bars
left = [1, 2, 3, 4, 5]

# heights of bars
height = [10, 24, 36, 40, 5]

# labels for bars
tick_label = ['one', 'two', 'three', 'four', 'five']

# plotting a bar chart
plt.bar(left, height, tick_label = tick_label,
                width = 0.8, color = ['red', 'green'])

# naming the x-axis
plt.xlabel('x - axis')
# naming the y-axis
plt.ylabel('y - axis')
# plot title
plt.title('My bar chart!')

# function to show the plot
plt.show()
```

Output:

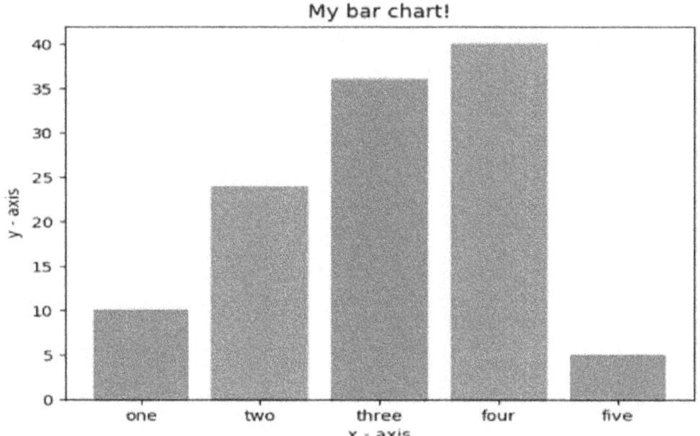

- Here, we use plt.bar() function to plot a bar chart.
- x-coordinates of left side of bars are passed along with heights of bars.

```python
from matplotlib import pyplot as plt
x = [5, 8, 10]
y = [12, 16, 6]
x2 = [6, 9, 11]
y2 = [6, 15, 7]
plt.bar(x, y, align = 'center')
plt.bar(x2, y2, color = 'g', align = 'center')
plt.title('Bar graph')
plt.ylabel('Y axis')
plt.xlabel('X axis')

plt.show()
```

## Output

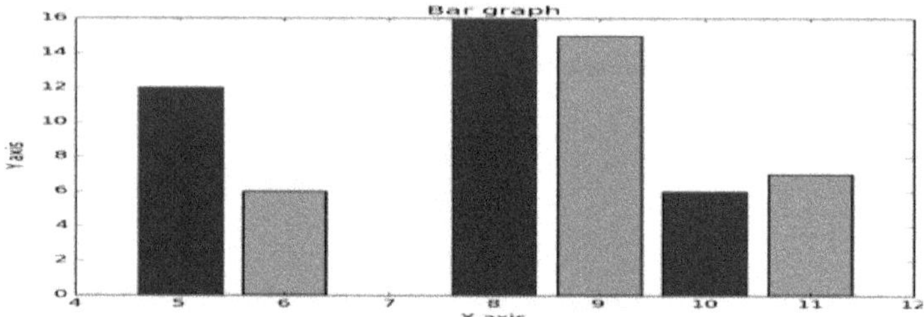

## 12.6 Scatter plot

```python
import matplotlib.pyplot as plt
# x-axis values
x = [1,2,3,4,5,6,7,8,9,10]
#y-axis values
y = [2,4,5,7,6,8,9,11,12,12]
#plotting points as a scatter plot
plt.scatter(x, y, label= "stars", color= "green",
                            marker= "*", s=30)
# x-axis label
plt.xlabel('x - axis')
#frequency label
plt.ylabel('y - axis')
#plot title
plt.title('My scatter plot!')
#showing legend
plt.legend()

#function to show the plot
plt.show()
```

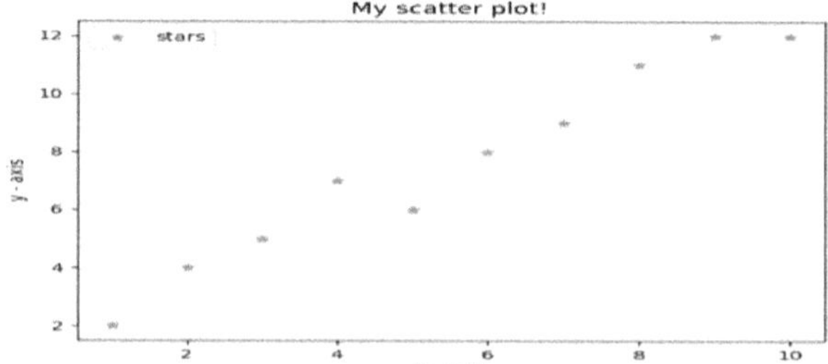

- Here, we use plt.scatter() function to plot a scatter plot.
- Like a line, we define x and corresponding y – axis values here as well.
- marker argument is used to set the character to use as marker. Its size can be defined using s parameter.

# CHAPTER XIII

## Data Structures and GUI, CGI Scripts

### 13.1 Python Standard Libraries

Standard libraries are used in programming languages to perform coding in an efficient manner. The Python Standard Library contains the exact syntax, semantics, and tokens of Python. It contains built-in modules that provide access to basic system functionality like I/O and some other core modules. Most of the Python Libraries are written in the C programming language. The Python standard library consists of more than 200 core modules. All these work together to make it a high-level programming language. The functionalities of Python can be accessed only by importing libraries.

**TensorFlow:** This library was developed by Google in collaboration with the Brain Team. It is an open-source library used for high-level computations. It is also used in machine learning and deep learning algorithms. It contains a large number of tensor operations. Researchers also use this Python library to solve complex computations in Mathematics and Physics.

1.  Matplotlib: This library is responsible for plotting numerical data. And that's why it is used in data analysis. It is also an open-source library and plots high-defined figures like pie charts, histograms, scatterplots, graphs, etc.
2.  Pandas: Pandas are an important library for data scientists. It is an open-source machine learning library that provides flexible high-level data structures and a variety of analysis tools. It eases data analysis, data manipulation, and cleaning of data. Pandas support operations like Sorting, Re-indexing, Iteration, Concatenation, Conversion of data, Visualizations, Aggregations, etc.
3.  Numpy: The name "Numpy" stands for "Numerical Python". It is the commonly used library. It is a popular machine learning library that supports large matrices and multi-

dimensional data. It consists of in-built mathematical functions for easy computations. Even libraries like TensorFlow use Numpy internally to perform several operations on tensors. Array Interface is one of the key features of this library.

4. SciPy: The name "SciPy" stands for "Scientific Python". It is an open-source library used for high-level scientific computations. This library is built over an extension of Numpy. It works with Numpy to handle complex computations. While Numpy allows sorting and indexing of array data, the numerical data code is stored in SciPy. It is also widely used by application developers and engineers.

5. Scrapy: It is an open-source library that is used for extracting data from websites. It provides very fast web crawling and high-level screen scraping. It can also be used for data mining and automated testing of data.

6. Scikit-learn: It is a famous Python library to work with complex data. Scikit-learn is an open-source library that supports machine learning. It supports variously supervised and unsupervised algorithms like linear regression, classification, clustering, etc. This library works in association with Numpy and SciPy.

7. PyGame: This library provides an easy interface to the Standard Directmedia Library (SDL) platform-independent graphics, audio, and input libraries. It is used for developing video games using computer graphics and audio libraries along with Python programming language.

8. PyTorch: PyTorch is the largest machine learning library that optimizes tensor computations. It has rich APIs to perform tensor computations with strong GPU acceleration. It also helps to solve application issues related to neural networks.

9. PyBrain: The name "PyBrain" stands for Python Based Reinforcement Learning, Artificial Intelligence, and Neural Networks library. It is an open-source library built for beginners in the field of Machine Learning. It provides fast and easy-to-use algorithms for machine learning tasks. It is

so flexible and easily understandable and that's why is really helpful for developers that are new in research fields.

Inorder to visualize the data we need to import the required liubraries according to our input and expected outcome.

Data visualization gives a elegant, organized pictorial representation of data which is easier to understand, interpret, observe and analyze.

It is visual form of representing data for understanding meaningful insight. It also provides correlations in variables. It can be visualized analyzed for better understanding.

Python provides different libraries with different features for visualizing data of different types. Those libraries come with different features and provide support for various types of graphs. Graphs always provide visual representation for easier understanding.

Here examples with Iris and Wine dataset are taken for better understanding on visualization.

*Import the essential packages*
*import pandas as pd*
*iris      =      pd.read_csv('iris.csv',      names=['sepal_length', 'sepal_width', 'petal_length', 'petal_width', 'class'])*
*print(iris.head())*

Output

|   | sepal_length | sepal_width | petal_length | petal_width | class |
|---|---|---|---|---|---|
| 0 | 5.1 | 3.5 | 1.4 | 0.2 | Iris-setosa |
| 1 | 4.9 | 3.0 | 1.4 | 0.2 | Iris-setosa |
| 2 | 4.7 | 3.2 | 1.3 | 0.2 | Iris-setosa |
| 3 | 4.6 | 3.1 | 1.5 | 0.2 | Iris-setosa |
| 4 | 5.0 | 3.6 | 1.4 | 0.2 | Iris-setosa |

## 13.2 Matplotlib

Matplotlib is the most popular Python plotting library. It is a low-level library with a Matlab-like interface that offers lots of freedom at the cost of having to write more code.

To install Matplotlib, pip, and conda can be used.

> *pip install matplotlib*
> *or*
> *conda install matplotlib*

Matplotlib is specifically suitable for creating basic graphs like line charts, bar charts, histograms, etc. It can be imported by typing:

> *import matplotlib.pyplot as plt*

## 13.3 Scatter Plot

To create a scatter plot in Matplotlib, we can use the scatter method. We also create a figure and an axis using plt.subplots to give our plot a title and labels.

```
# create a figure and axis
fig, ax = plt.subplots()
# scatter the sepal_length against the sepal_width
ax.scatter(iris['sepal_length'], iris['sepal_width'])
# set a title and labels
ax.set_title('Iris Dataset')
ax.set_xlabel('sepal_length')
ax.set_ylabel('sepal_width')
```

OUTPUT

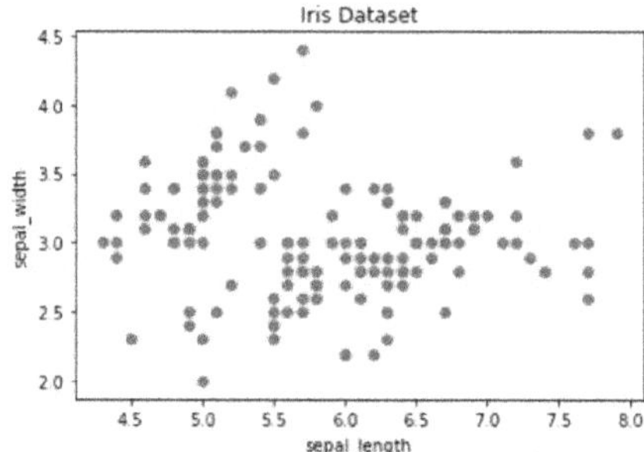

  We can give the graph more meaning by coloring each data point
by its class. This can be done by creating a dictionary that maps
from class to color and then scattering each point on its own using
a for-loop and passing the respective color.

```
# create color dictionary
colors = {'Iris-setosa':'r', 'Iris-versicolor':'g', 'Iris-virginica':'b'}
# create a figure and axis
fig, ax = plt.subplots()
# plot each data-point
for i in range(len(iris['sepal_length'])):
    ax.scatter(iris['sepal_length'][i],
iris['sepal_width'][i],color=colors[iris['class'][i]])
# set a title and labels
ax.set_title('Iris Dataset')
ax.set_xlabel('sepal_length')
ax.set_ylabel('sepal_width')
```

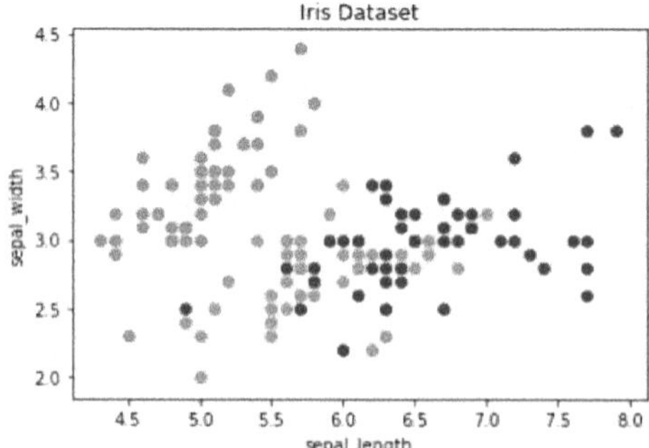

## 13.4 Line Chart

In Matplotlib, we can create a line chart by calling the plot method. We plot multiple columns in one graph by looping through the columns and plotting each column on the same axis.

```
# get columns to plot
columns = iris.columns.drop(['class'])
# create x data
x_data = range(0, iris.shape[0])
# create figure and axis
fig, ax = plt.subplots()
# plot each column
for column in columns:
    ax.plot(x_data, iris[column])
# set title and legend
ax.set_title('Iris Dataset')
ax.legend()
```

OUTPUT

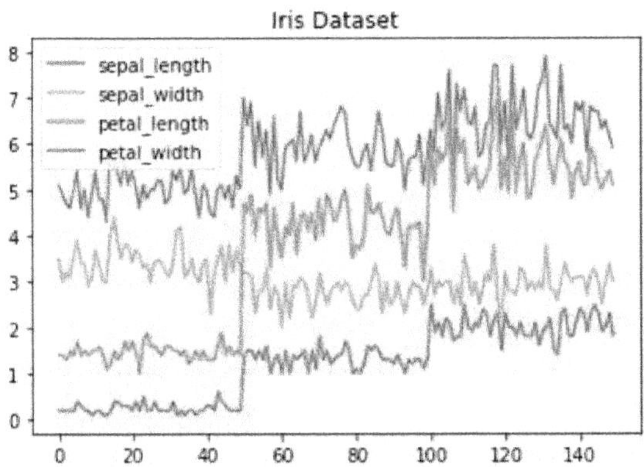


 In Matplotlib, we can create a Histogram using the hist method. If we pass categorical data like the points column from the wine-review dataset, it will automatically calculate how often each class occurs.

```
# create figure and axis
fig, ax = plt.subplots()
# plot histogram
ax.hist(wine_reviews['points'])
# set title and labels
ax.set_title('Wine Review Scores')
ax.set_xlabel('Points')
ax.set_ylabel('Frequency')
```

OUTPUT

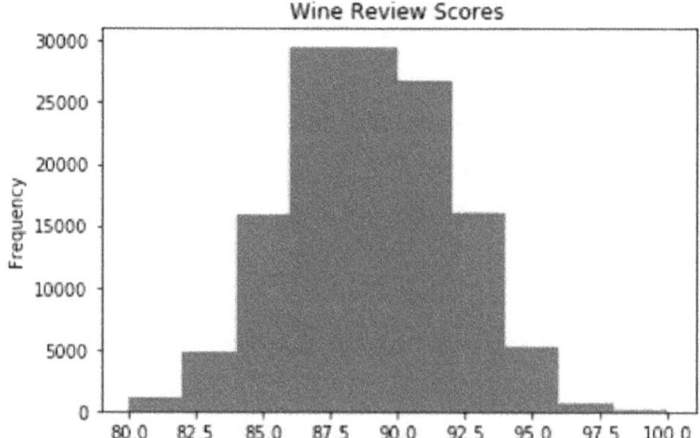


## 13.5 Bar Chart

A bar chart can be created using the bar method. The bar chart isn't automatically calculating the frequency of a category, so we will use pandas value_counts method to do this. The bar chart is useful for categorical data that doesn't have a lot of different categories (less than 30) because else it can get quite messy.

```
# create a figure and axis
fig, ax = plt.subplots()
# count the occurrence of each class
data = wine_reviews['points'].value_counts()
# get x and y data
points = data.index
frequency = data.values
```

```
# create bar chart
ax.bar(points, frequency)
# set title and labels
ax.set_title('Wine Review Scores')
ax.set_xlabel('Points')
ax.set_ylabel('Frequency')
```

OUTPUT

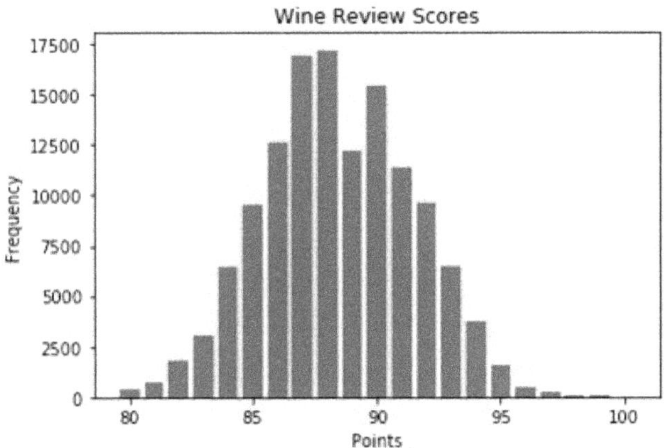


## 13.6 Pandas Visualization

Pandas is an open-source, high-performance, and easy-to-use library providing data structures, such as data frames and data analysis tools like the visualization tools we will use in this article.

Pandas Visualization makes it easy to create plots out of a pandas dataframe and series. It also has a higher-level API than Matplotlib, and therefore we need less code for the same results.

Pandas can be installed using either pip or conda.

*pip install pandas*
*or*
*conda install pandas*